GONE TO BLAZES!

ONE MAN'S EXPERIENCE AS A FIREFIGHTER AND
HIS WITNESS TO GOVERNMENT VANDALISM

BRUCE WILKINSON

Gone To Blazes!
Copyright © 2022 by Bruce Wilkinson

All rights reserved. No part of this publication may be reproduced, distributed, or transmitted in any form or by any means, including photocopying, recording, or other electronic or mechanical methods, without the prior written permission of the author, except in the case of brief quotations embodied in critical reviews and certain other non-commercial uses permitted by copyright law.

Tellwell Talent
www.tellwell.ca

ISBN
978-0-2288-7490-4 (Paperback)
978-0-2288-7491-1 (eBook)

Introduction.

I SERVED IN THE FIRE SERVICE IN BRISBANE, initially in the Brisbane Metropolitan Fire Brigade and after in the Queensland Fire service from 1967 until my retirement in 2002, making 35 years service. During my time in operational service I was able to make progress through the ranks, eventually reaching the rank of station officer first class, at the same time experiencing the best and the worst that this profession can give you.

As I was elected to the leadership of the officers union there was a change in government with the new ALP Queensland government expecting all trade unions to give service to their party. People who demonstrated their willingness to abide by this policy were promoted to senior positions, meaning within a short time the fire service was controlled by the director-general appointed by the government down through the compliant senior officers.

As I was more inclined to serve the public and the men I worked with, sometimes putting me in conflict with the government and their agencies, I became a target to be eliminated if possible. Nevertheless, I survived and I was able to watch the departure of some of the people who wanted me gone, eventually retiring at a time of my own choosing.

This book is an account of my experiences on active duty, my interchange with officers both good and bad, my conflict with bureaucracy, and the price that the fire service has had to pay since it became managed by the Queensland government.

Glossary of terms.

Acting positions. When a senior officer is absent on sick leave or some other cause, the rank immediately beneath him may be given the opportunity to act at this rank level. It is sometimes referred to as "acting up", but does not mean any kind of bad behaviour.

BA board. This is a board positioned beside a fire engine at an emergency, and it shows any fire staff wearing breathing apparatus, their names, when they began to wear it, the number of the breathing apparatus set, and when they are due to report back to the fire appliance.

K PA/PSI. These are terms used to show pressures, usually on breathing apparatus or pump gauges showing water pressure. K PA is an abbreviation for kilopascals; the metric system for pressure measurement. PSI means pounds per square inch; the imperial measure for pressure. One pound per square inch is equal to approximately 7 kPa.

Appliances. A wide variety of emergency vehicles are commonly referred to as appliances. They may be suburban fire engines, aerial equipment, or any other specialist appliance.

Aerials. These are appliances used to gain access to high levels. There are two varieties, turntable ladders and hydraulic platforms. A turntable ladder is mounted on the rear of a specialist vehicle and the ladder itself is controlled by the road motor through a series of mechanical transfers. Turntable ladders can extend to 40 metres or more. A hydraulic platform is a square platform surrounded by security guard rails and again controlled and extended by the road motor. Both of these aerial appliances can be used for life rescue or directing water onto a fire.

Pumps. This usually refers to fire engines that would attend fires. They are also referred to sometimes as pumpers. It also refers to the pump mounted on the vehicle and used to control water flow.

BA. This is a breathing apparatus worn by firefighters under any circumstances where the atmosphere could be toxic, including fires and gas leaks. Breathing apparatus sets these days are open circuit compressed air sets similar in operation to diving sets.

Resuscitation. This is a process used to revive somebody who has been overcome by smoke, toxic gases or anything else that has caused them to lose a pulse and stop breathing. It involves a routine compression of the chest to force the heart to pump blood through the body and breathing air into the mouth of the patient to provide oxygen to the lungs. It is often referred to in the fire service as "resus".

Ambu manikin. This looks like a fashion model dummy without the bottom half of the body. It is specially constructed so that any firefighter in training can apply resuscitation to the Ambu manikin and it will demonstrate whether his efforts are good enough to revive a patient.

Proto. This was an old breathing apparatus set that used oxygen directly to the wearer. Expelled carbon dioxide gas from the wearer was removed through a chemical process within the set. This was a closed circuit set; it is now and has been for some time, a museum piece.

Oxy vivas. These are sets carried on all fire appliances and can also be found on all ambulances. They are designed to administer oxygen at a predetermined level to a patient until the patient is transported to hospital.

PA. This is the radio system carried on all fire service vehicles and connected directly to our communication centre. Every vehicle has a number and will call the communication centre identifying itself and the person making the call, giving the information about the reason for moving, e.g. destination, before it moves. Similarly, it will "book in" to the communication centre on arrival. At emergency incidents every decision, every action, is reported to the communication centre through the PA. PA of course means public address; if necessary the radio system can be used to address the public at an emergency.

CBD. This means the central business district, encompassing that area from the river down to fortitude Valley and from Roma Street Station to the QUT.

Chem unit. The Chem unit was an initiative of the Queensland University of technology and was designed to educate all emergency service personnel about different chemical emergencies, what actions should be taken, and the role of each emergency service at such an incident.

UFU. This is the United firefighters union, representing all professional rank and file firefighters.

AWU. This is the Australian workers union, who had firefighters among their membership until it lost the right to represent them to the United firefighters union.

MFBOA. This is the Metropolitan Fire Brigade officers Association. It was a registered union body representing officers in the Brisbane Metropolitan Fire Brigade. It disappeared when it was amalgamated with the United firefighters union by means of a rigged Ball.

Dedication

This book is dedicated to all fire fighters who confront emergencies without fear or favour, and especially to those who have paid the ultimate price.

Table of Contents

Introduction. iii
Glossary of terms. iv
Dedication.. vii
Chapter 1. In the beginning-------- 1
Chapter 2. The United firefighters union..............................17
Chapter 3. Promotion..19
Chapter 4. Amalgamation. 26
Chapter 5. Victimisation, discrimination and harassment. 32
Chapter 6. Other innocent victims. 46
Chapter 7. The Terrible Tragedy...52
Chapter 8. Gender (In) equality. 55
Chapter 9. Mundingburra..58
Chapter 10. The Vanishing File..62
Chapter 11. The pre-scripted promotion saga. 65
Chapter 12. The Underground Newspaper. 68
Chapter 13. The Counterfeit Commissioner..........................70
Chapter 14. Fire service legislation (the vandalism of) 74
Chapter 15. Smoke Alarm Fiasco. 77
Chapter 16. Grand Larceny. 81
Chapter 17. Interesting Jobs. 88
Chapter 18. A Fire Service Review (before and after). 92
Chapter 19. A Summary. 97

Chapter 1. In the beginning-------

NO, THIS IS NOT A REWRITE OF THE OLD TESTAMENT. This is my beginning in the Brisbane Metropolitan Fire Brigade in 1967.

It began with months of intensive training and education. Drills in the yard learning every possible position, each position having a different set of duties, each fire action different from the last and needing different responses from each member of the crew. The end result of training was to produce a fire crew on any pump that would operate at a single command like an integrated well-oiled machine. Every fire appliance had equipment stowed in different lockers and every recruit had to learn where to find each piece of equipment, what it was used for, and how to put it into operation. Every piece of equipment was numbered; every piece of equipment had a history card; every length of hose was graded. This numbering and identification process included fire staff. Every fireman had his own number. My number was 114.

Lectures were given to explain hydraulics, the operations of different pumps, energy changes from a water main or a static supply of water through the pump to the hose.

Within a few weeks I realised that I was in the right place for me; I felt like I belonged.

Training continued for three months learning everything that could possibly make us useful as an operational firefighter. This included different methods of rescue including carrying down on a ladder. This was done from the third platform of the tower at Kemp Place in Brisbane. The third platform was approximately 30 feet or nine metres above the ground and when the gates were open there was nothing between the platform floor and fresh air. We would be paired and sent aloft to the platform. One of us would be told to lie down on the floor; he was unconscious. The other would be told to pick him up, position him over his shoulders, mount a ladder and carry him down to the ground.

Rescuing a workmate.

It was a difficult operation for both parties. Lying over somebody's shoulders looking at the concrete while he descends, Rolling his shoulders is a challenging experience. I have seen a number of patients being rescued suddenly regain consciousness and climb back up the ladder.

Part of our training included breathing apparatus training at the old Ann Street fire station. The Department that operated there was known as Safety Equipment. They were responsible for all types of breathing apparatus, resuscitation equipment, gas testing devices and all kinds of rescue equipment. As new recruits we went to the safety equipment department for our first introduction to the wearing of breathing apparatus. This involved instruction on the equipment, how it works and how to clean it and put it back up for duty, followed by our first experience in heat and smoke. There was a room about the size of a double garage with a tunnel constructed of timber around three sides. This tunnel, we were to learn, was stacked in various places with bags of sawdust blocking the passage. The walls of this room were black, not from paint but from smoke, which was piped into this room whenever breathing apparatus was about to be used. There was no control over the temperature or humidity. This was before the days of generated artificial smoke. Outside the door was a large red button. This was connected to the ambulance station next door. If anybody went down and was dragged out the button would be hit and the ambulance would respond. The breathing apparatus we wore in those days was a closed circuit set; that is it had a chemical in it to remove the expelled carbon dioxide from your breath.

A gas test with breathing apparatus.

Consequently, because of this chemical reaction, it got hot. Once you were wearing your breathing apparatus, you entered the tunnel working in pairs. You had to move the bags in the tunnel so that you could proceed, one partner passing a bag to his partner behind. There was really no visibility, and it seemed to me to be even hotter inside the tunnel. Every operational fireman (this was what we were called then, the gender neutral term of firefighter had not been adopted) did a number of "refresher BAs" per year. Inside the tunnel was no place for claustrophobics. I have seen refresher crews, at the finish of their refresher, lean over the rail outside the BA room and not move for five minutes. Anybody rostered for a refresher got no other duties for that day.

More of our training at safety equipment involved the use of gas testing devices and resuscitation equipment. "Resus" was learned using an 'ambu mannequin'—a special dummy that would teach you whether or not your external cardiac compression and mouth-to-mouth resuscitation was good enough to save a life. The gas testing devices were there to alert you to the presence of many of the toxic and fatal gases that could be encountered in this profession.

Over time, Safety Equipment was moved to become a separate section at Roma Street Station. The training area now was designed like a ship with different decks and hatches and an engine room. There was even an escape tunnel from the engine room up to the top deck as you would find on ships. The smoke became artificial smoke and the conditions were controlled; temperature, humidity, et cetera. The Protos that we used to wear (closed circuit oxygen sets) became museum pieces and we wore open circuit compressed air sets. Oxy-Vivas became standard equipment and resuscitation became more sophisticated.

Initial training had a wide area. Obviously, the fire service needed to establish that we were not frightened of heights. This meant that we had to do a height test on a turntable ladder, up to a height of 80 feet or about 24 metres. When you first approach the base of a turntable ladder you are reassured. It is wide, solid, strong, immovable. You mount with confidence. The problem is, each section of that ladder has to fit into the one below it, therefore each progressive section has to be smaller than the one below it. By the time you get to the top, the section you're standing on reminds you of your childhood experience with a Meccano set. You reassure yourself that you can look below at the appliance that the ladder is mounted on and regain that mental confidence. When you look down, you learn that the appliance, because of the angle of the ladder, is in fact well behind you and you are looking directly at the concrete. If you happen to be there on a windy day, you learn that this little, flimsy section of ladder that you're standing on is indeed affected by the wind, and you will wave to and fro. You are expected of course, to demonstrate your self-confidence by instructing the operator at the base of the ladder through the walkie-talkie at the head of the ladder to carry out certain operations; left revolve, right revolve, depress ladder, elevate ladder, et cetera in a voice that sounds confident.

A hose line in action.

Once our instructors believed that we knew enough about pump operation, we were given pump operation for real; wet stuff. This involved running out hose, putting a pump into operation, showing that you could handle a line of hose under normal operational pressure (about 600 kPa or 80 psi), showing that you could understand what the gauges at the pump were telling you and that you could change the pressures and predict what your limitations would be with your existing water supply.

At the end of your training there was an exam. In fact, there were four exams, three written and one practical. Mathematics, English and general knowledge, to show that you retained some of the stuff that you'd been listening to, and a practical exam in the yard to show that you could perform practically in a crew at a fire ground. If you passed these exams, you were then a third class fireman. This meant that you had started on your climb through the ranks. It meant many other things. It meant that you are now riding a fire appliance with an officer and other firemen with much more experience and a higher rank than you. It meant that you had to heed their advice and instructions and learn. It meant that your pay was set at third class fireman's pay according to the award. It meant that you were now working shift work; the fire service works 24 hours a day seven days a week. It is an essential emergency service.

First thing in the morning on a dayshift, all staff would assemble in the yard for an exercise routine to music. The music was titled "the dance of the honeybees". We were known as the hairy fairies.

Once you had clambered onto this first wrung of the fire service structure, you were ushered into the Chief Officer's office. He read the names of his new recruits, spoke to you briefly, and said, "if you appear in my office again it will probably mean that you're in trouble." The Chief Officer, when I joined the fire brigade, was George Healy. I learned over time that Chief Officer Healy was a truly remarkable man. I encountered him in the station some years later and he greeted me with "Hello Bruce, how are the boys?" At a major fire, he made sure that he knew where everybody was and how long they had been there. On one occasion at a major factory fire, I was on a line of hose with another man about halfway into the factory with less than one metre of ceiling space, on my gut. I felt a hand on my shoulder and turned my head to see Chief Officer George Healy, asking who he had there and how long we had been there, after which he wriggled back out. Not long after we were relieved with a fresh branch crew. If the government of the day needed advice about an emergency, Chief Officer Healy would be contacted; not by a bureaucrat, not by a government minister, but by the Premier.

The shift work at that time involved six days straight. The first two days were from 3 PM till 11 PM, the second two were from 11 PM till 7 AM (known as the quick change, only eight hours between finish and start), and the last two were from 11 PM till 7 AM. Lectures and training continued all through working life for all ranks.

As you gained experience and more knowledge, after a year as a third class fireman you could sit for a second class fireman's exam, which was the same format as the first exam but of a higher standard. Each passing year gave you the opportunity to advance to a higher rank by examination; second class, first-class C grade, first class B grade, and first-class A grade.

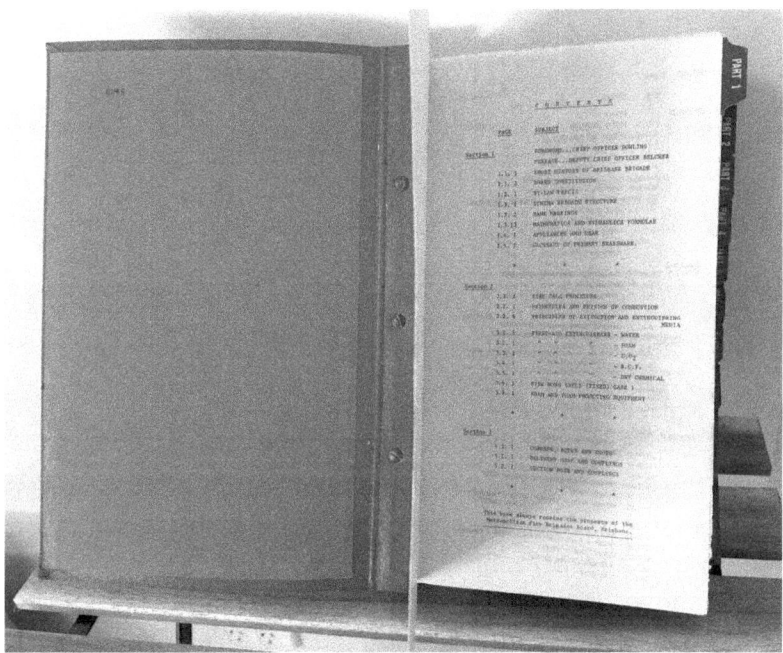

A peak inside the book.

The book of knowledge. What every firefighter needs to learn.

At this point in working life, you had to decide whether to remain in the fireman's ranks (most men did) or attempt to gain officer rank with much more responsibility.

If you chose this course, it would involve several months of intense study preparing for examinations both practical and theoretical of a high standard.

A diploma in frontline Management.

It is obvious, when you look at the rank structure and the crews on appliances, there is a need for more firemen than officers. A lot of men sat for the officer's exam and failed. They were good fireman. This simply means it is a difficult hurdle to get over.

I learned a lot during this period of my employment from officers I worked with, both good and bad. A good officer would try to relate to his troops, making sure they made progress and gaining their support. Bad officers were generally in my opinion somewhat insecure and they relied on their rank to order people around. Firemen working with bad officers usually did only what they had to do. Good officers, on the other hand, would get the complete support from their crew, above and beyond what was required. It was obvious to me, if I achieved officer rank, which category I should fall into. In any sort of emergency, major fire, motor vehicle accident or something else, although the decisions as an officer may be yours, if you don't listen to the rest of your crew and make use of their knowledge and experience, you're a damn fool.

There is another part of this relationship between officers and men, and I will give a couple of examples of how this might play out. There was an officer at the old Woolloongabba fire station who was particularly disliked. The other thing I can remember about this officer was that he was terrified of his wife. This was a lady who liked to cook, especially at Christmas time. The officer had ordered several dozen eggs for his wife's culinary efforts. They were stacked in the messroom to be taken home and delivered to the lady of the house at the termination of his shift. The messroom had a large tea urn. These eggs were carefully placed in the urn for about 20 minutes and then placed back in the containers to be delivered to the demon cook. It must've been a very interesting Christmas in that household.

Another officer at Kemp Place made a point of ordering everybody upstairs for a lecture in the evenings and placing himself in one of the deck chairs in front of the television set. He became predictable; always came at the same time, always sat in the same chair. On this particular night, a fairly large fireworks bunger (in those days you could buy fireworks at the paper shop) was carefully taped under the chair and a lighted cigarette taped to the wick. Right on cue, the shift was ordered upstairs to the lecture room. Everybody waited a few minutes for the explosion that followed. The said officer never invaded the messroom again.

The first level of officer was Substation Officer. These men took charge of outstations with one pump and a crew. When these outstations responded to an alarm, decisions at these emergencies was the Substation Officer's as was the responsibility for the outcome. Pay was fortnightly, in cash, all correctly allocated in envelopes marked with the name and number of each fireman and sealed by the paymaster. The appropriate envelopes were sent to the outstations and each outstation had a safe to secure this money, the responsibility of the Substation Officer.

Station time was well organised, you might say regimented. There was allocated lecture time, drill time, gear cleaning time and station duties, which involved cleaning and polishing everything in the station and the station itself. Appliance drivers were responsible for their vehicles, cleaning everything on the pump and in the pump so that every vehicle shone like a decoration on a Christmas tree.

Our principal responsibility, in fact the reason for our existence, was to respond to emergencies; to rescue the public and to save their property.

Rescuing a child.

This responsibility was taken very seriously. When an alarm went off, everybody ran to their appliances; we were expected to be out the door within 30 seconds of the alarm. Arrival at the incident should occur within three minutes of alarm time. If you didn't make it in that time, there would be a senior officer asking you what the hell went wrong. Our badge at that time had a motto, "Semper Paratus", which means "always ready". We worked by that motto.

The watch room—the source of all fire alarms—was attached to the old Ann Street fire station. It was a fairly large room with a desk in the middle containing two phones, two books, a daily diary and an occurrence book. Anything and everything that took place was carefully noted down in the occurrence book. The four walls were full of little squares with a switch under each square. Each square housed an alarm connected to a building in the city. If any alarm operated, the watchroom officer would turn out the appropriate station with all the relevant information for the alarm. In Kemp Place, this would mean a turnout of two pumps, very often having the senior officer on duty riding the second pump. Pumps were not governed and travelled at speed to the alarm. Nevertheless, the fire brigade had a much better accident record than the rest of the community.

When I joined the fire brigade, on-shift firemen were an interesting mix. There were some hard men among them. Returned men from the Second World War, Tobruk Rats, New Guinea jungle fighters, as well as ordinary tradesmen; men who were physically capable and good with their hands. There were disputes between individuals that were sometimes settled in the light well; a small open area adjacent to the messroom.

We were issued with appropriate clothing for our various areas of responsibility. We had denims for everyday work in the station, and we had the all-important protective clothing to wear to fires. A turnout coat consisted of very heavy woollen serge, and it served us well. It protected us from heat, it did not burn easily, it got wet very often and dried out again. It was worn with a heavy belt which carried a beltline, high-quality cord to be applied to hose lines or anything else, and a fireman's axe. I don't think I have ever been to a major structural fire where I did not use my fireman's axe. There was a clothing issue allocated to each fireman and if you needed something outside that you needed approval of a senior officer.

At the time I joined the fire service, we were issued with brass helmets. The turnout coats had brass buttons and all of this brass was expected to be clean and shiny all the time. We were issued with leather work boots as well as leather top boots. Top boots came up to the top of your shin and they were what was worn when you needed to get dressed in a hurry at night. Once a week on afternoon shift, after a lot of gear cleaning time, there was a full dress inspection on parade. All of this clothing (brass, axe, boots) had to be sparkling.

There was a disciplinary process similar to what you might find in similar organisations with a rank structure. Charges could be made against any fireman for any misbehaviour, and such matters would be addressed by the Chief Officer. Complaints by rank and file firemen could be heard by the Chief Officer or his deputy. There was also a shop steward on every shift at the major stations. If there was a serious issue, the shift would meet and discuss it and direct their concerns to the shop steward who could approach the Chief Officer. It meant that concerns could be aired and settled quickly and it worked very well.

If there was a serious problem that affected all fire staff the industrial union could refer the matter to the Industrial Commission, where submissions and evidence could be heard and the Commission could adjudicate on the matter.

The Fireman's messroom contained everything needed for preparing a meal; stove top, oven, sink, fridge, and of course, tables and chairs. Every fireman contributed on a fortnightly basis to the fireman's req club, which in turn provided the messroom with the daily paper and a TV set.

These facilities were duplicated upstairs; at major stations like Kemp Place the firemen occupied the ground floor and the officers the floor above. Immediately inside the door of the station, across from the foyer, was the duty office. The duty officer, assisted by the PA system and telephone links to the communication centre (then known as the watch room) controlled the every day operations in the station. Immediately behind the duty office was the key room. Every alarm connected to the fire service supplied us with a key to the premises. This meant that all of those keys (and there were many) were housed in a secure key room controlled by the communication centre. In the event of an alarm to one of the premises protected by a fire alarm system, the communication centre broadcast through PA the name and address of the premises, and the number of the keys to those premises. The duty officer would now be able to enter the key room (unlocked at this time by the Communications Centre) and retrieve the identified keys to the premises for the responding pump.

The positioning of fire appliances was intended to give the people of Brisbane the best emergency protection the fire brigade could arrange. Kemp Place, the station beside the North entrance of the Story Bridge, had three pumps as well as other special appliances. Roma Street Station, adjacent to Roma Street railway station, also had three pumps. Windsor station and Woolloongabba Station, later to become Annerley station, both had two pumps. All other outstations had one pump. What is referred to here as a pump is what the public recognises as a fire engine that would arrive at an emergency; a fire, motor vehicle accident et cetera.

The major stations, Kemp Place and Roma St also had special appliances. These included turntable ladders and hydraulic platforms for high angle rescue and a salvage van containing a wide variety of equipment for rescue work, including different kinds of stretchers.

This positioning of appliances was designed to ensure that every suburb had a pump available at all times. If Chermside station was turned out to an emergency, the second pump from Windsor would move towards Chermside station. If the pump from Chermside needed help at their emergency, the second pump from Windsor was already halfway there and could respond under siren. If not, Windsor's second pump would man Chermside station until they returned. If, during this turnout time, the remaining pump at Windsor was called to an emergency, the third pump from Kemp Place, known as "the flyer", would move towards Windsor station. This positioning of appliances and standby system meant that Brisbane had the best possible protection that the Brisbane Metropolitan Fire Brigade could arrange.

Pumps at this time were open, that is, they had no roof. This meant that in bad weather, if you were turned out, you got wet whether there was a fire or not. These pumps had an electric bell mounted on the front with a large hand-operated bell on the passenger side of the front seat. These warning devices were operated vigourously at every intersection.

Working night shift was a totally different experience. If an alarm occurred in the middle of the night, alarm bells would ring, the lights would come on (these are known as the detent lights), and the crews would scramble as quickly as possible to their respective appliances. The Communication centre broadcasts a wake-up call at 6 AM. This is normally a quick reference to time over the PA. There was one lady in the communication centre who adopted her own wake-up system. She would simply open the PA and give out a series of orgasmic moans. The effect that this would have on a bunch of fit firemen first thing in the morning could be, shall we say, orgasmic.

Outstation Life.

After you had served some time in the city and had demonstrated your competence, you could be transferred to an outstation. Outstation duty was different but fairly consistent. On duty was an officer and three, sometimes two, firemen. As a crew, they were responsible for cleaning the station and the pump, testing and recording all equipment, and responding to requests from the local community. We would attend local fetes and special school days. Sometimes the outstation would receive a request from the local police station to attend some display with them. District knowledge was paramount. So that you could make as rapid a response as possible, you needed to know the area; the streets, the parks, the major buildings, as soon as you received an alarm.

Forced Entry!

At the change of shift, it was necessary to ensure that the oncoming shift did indeed arrive in total. If somebody was late or was not coming, someone on the offgoing shift had to remain until that vacancy was filled. This was an emergency service that had to be able to respond on a minute's notice.

When the pump responded to an emergency, the officer had to make some quick decisions:---

1. What immediate action to take.
2. If it was a fire, what exposures need to be protected.
3. Are all civilians accounted for or is there a need for rescue.
4. 4. Give word back on the radio giving an accurate description of the circumstances, what action has been taken, is the situation under control, and what if any assistance is required. This may include a request for the attendance of other services; e.g. police and ambulance.

Attendance at a structural fire for an outstation crew is extremely demanding for all personnel; they are personally reassured in their mind that a back up pump and crew is close at hand.

In 1967 there were 18 fire stations in Brisbane. As the city grew, this expanded slowly to 21 stations. This expansion ceased when the fire service was taken over by the government.

Trade union stuff.

Chapter 2. The United firefighters union.

IN 1967, the United Firefighters Union was not registered. The registered union for fire staff was the Australian Workers Union. The United Firefighters Union (UFU) was beginning a long fight to gain recognition. I was a foundation member of the UFU in 1967. During my training period there was a strike by fire staff. They were carrying out what was called "fire calls only". This was brought about by the actions of the **board** against a fireman, Darcy McCarthy. There was a strict rule by the board against fireman working on their days off in any other job. McCarthy was running a driving school, and the board hired a private detective, whose wife took driving lessons from McCarthy. When the board had all the evidence they needed, McCarthy's employment was terminated. The fire staff rallied to his defence, hence the strike. It was in fact common practice for fireman to do some extra work on their days off to pay the bills, me included. Eventually, the matter was decided in the Industrial Commission where it was agreed that the penalty (his dismissal) was much too harsh and he had to be reinstated.

In these early days of the late 60s and early 70s, trade unionism and industrial relations was an area I knew almost nothing about. There were union meetings in the station which we all attended, but that was about the limit of our participation and knowledge. I do remember in the early 70s sitting in an office adjacent to the Fireman's messroom at Kemp Place with Arthur Rogers working on the 10- 14 roster. This was a roster that would eventually replace our current working hours. It meant working two ten-hour days followed by two 14 hour nights. Each man had to work the required number of hours per week, there were four shifts so we had to have the necessary number of men at any time on each shift and we had to make sure that the whole thing balanced out and did not break any rules. The new shift meant that fireman would be working an average 42 hours a week. In order to correct this, a "Z" shift was created; this was a separate shift designed to repay the extra two hours. Every on-shift man had a "Z" number; when anyone's Z number came up on the shift day he took a day off and he was replaced by one of the Z shift. Arthur and I spent many hours working the numbers until we were satisfied we had something to submit to the Chief Officer.

By the time the 1014 was adopted (late 70s) I was able to negotiate the finer points with Chief Officer Belcher; e.g. meal break times. If you started work at 18:00 hours and you took that forward four hours it would mean that you'd have your meal break at 22.00 hours. We agreed to combine the two breaks and have them at 20:30 hours.

Once the union was registered, there was a power grab; interested parties wanted control of the new registered union. Eventually, Arthur Rogers was kicked out and the left faction gained control of the United Firefighters Union.

Chapter 3. Promotion.

THE METROPOLITAN FIRE BRIGADE OFFICERS ASSOCIATION.

I managed to achieve sub-station Officer rank by 1975.

My officer's cap.

This meant that I would now leave the UFU and become a member of the above-named union (MFBOA). This was a union small in number (less than 200) but democratic and caring of its members.

The union ran a separate account; a sick fund that would support any member who was off sick/incapacitated for a long time beyond his allocated sick pay. When necessary, all union members would contribute to support the incapacitated member who would be paid 50% of his normal weekly pay. There were occasions when an injured man was supported for an extensive period of time until he was fit to return to work.

Within a short time I became president of this union. Little did I know that it would cause me all sorts of problems. It coincided with the merging of all fire brigades into the Queensland Fire and Rescue Service. It meant we were no longer dealing with a Chief Officer and the Board, but we were dealing with the Queensland government, bureaucrats, and all the other disadvantages that come with a government department.

We were soon under the authority of a Labor government, and this government believed that all trade unions should be compliant with the government. If the decisions of the fire service management and the government were wrong, I believed it was my responsibility to say so, often publically. This put me out of favour with the director-general, who was now running the fire service, and I became a target, to be removed and replaced if possible.

An early QFSbadge acknowledging Brisbane.

My first conflict with the government was with the Minister for Emergency Services, Martin Tenni. I was stationed at the time at Ithaca fire station, but I had moved down to Roma Street for the day so that I could attend a meeting with Bluey O'Gorman from the Police Union. When I returned to Roma Street Station I was approached by several firemen, expressing concern about the state of the first appliance. When I opened the door and looked in the cabin, I was able to look straight through the floor at the concrete. The floor had been rusted out. This was an appliance not fit for fire service duty. In fact this vehicle would probably be put off the road by the police if it was in ordinary commercial use.

This was the first response pump to the CBD, including Parliament house, Martin Tenni's workplace.

I telephoned Channel 7 and spoke to Chris Adams, who ran a program called Today Tonight. Chris came down to the station and we did an interview to be aired that night, including exposure of the cabin floor. This was my first encounter with Chris Adams. Of all the journalists I encountered over the next few years, he was certainly the best. He was very good at his profession, I found I could trust him, and he was a great source of information.

To say that Tenni was unhappy would be an understatement. He was outraged. He had an urgent meeting with Wally Belcher and demanded some sort of retaliation. Chief Officer Belcher visited Roma Street station the following day to give a fairly stern lecture to the shift. Back at Ithaca station, I received several phone calls from fire staff at Roma Street about the visit. Considering that I was responsible for the events, I felt I should not be hiding away in an outstation. I rang the senior officer, Stuart Thompson, a man I liked and respected, and said basically, "this isn't right I'll come down there." "No, no, no" said Stewy "you stay up there". I understood his response and had a chuckle.

I received an advice from the Chief Officer telling me that I was to be reprimanded. Some weeks later I called him to tell him that I was travelling to Mount Cootha for an interview. He said, "you're not in uniform are you?" I replied no, but on the way back I can call into your office and get that reprimand. Once in his office, just the two of us, he said, "if you repeat any of this I'll deny I said it".

Apparently, Tenni had demanded that I be charged with doing a television interview in brigade time. The Chief Officer told him I was on my lunch hour. He demanded that I be charged for allowing television crews in the station. The Chief Officer told him that it was done on the apron (that area between the building and the road). Tenni replied, "you charge him with something or I will sack you".

I survived. Chief officer Wally Belcher did what he had to do to survive himself, at the same time trying not to do me any damage.

Chief Officer Belcher eventually became the Queensland Fire Service's first Commissioner, a position he held until ill-health forced him out of the position. He had confided in me on one occasion, "I can't stay any longer." Long after he retired, we communicated frequently. Mindful of his health, I was always concerned that perhaps I should leave him alone, but when I spoke to his wife on the phone and said I would understand if he was not able to take the call, she replied, "he will want to talk to you."

It soon became obvious to me that I was not likely to command much attention from the media because I represented a very small number of people. I needed a bigger crowd, more clout. I made some approaches to associated emergency services and put together an organisation called the Combined Professional Emergency Services Organisation, combining the unions of the police, the ambulance, fire staff and nurses. Suddenly together we represented many thousands. I was immediately able to book an interview with the Australian Broadcasting Corporation (ABC), conducted at their old studio at Toowong. I have to say it wasn't all that difficult; after all we had a Conservative government and this was the ABC. We put together an interview in the studio representing all of the emergency services and making the public aware of what we saw as serious shortfalls in our resources. The interviewer was a lady called Donna Meiklejohn. I remember at the end of the interview she said to me, "we'd better get that make up off you before you get some propositions, and it won't be from the girls".

These developments changed behaviour within the fire service itself. We still had a chief officer and a board. If you had good cause, you could approach and communicate with the Chief Officer but the board and certainly the chairman of the board was out of reach. I received a phone call from the chairman of the board inviting me to contact him at any time about any issue. He gave me his personal phone number as well as another number which I assume was for another residence. This was unprecedented. The Chairman of the board at the time was a man named Gordon Olive. Suddenly we were chatting away like old friends; it was Gordon and Bruce, very informal. I believe this was brought about by a combination of factors; the television interviews involving all emergency services created a lot of attention, and the fact that the normally conservative chairman of the board and I were suddenly faced with a common enemy, threatening the good maintenance of the fire service.

During the 1980s I made many interviews, covering every channel at different times. At least one press conference and media releases were delivered frequently.

During this period I also attended a National conference in Wodonga in Victoria. This was a conference attended by representatives of every firefighter's union in Australia, and in this case, also two men from New Zealand. The purpose of this conference was to discuss and promote fire service standards from state to state and the possibility of interstate support. I was elected as the chair of this conference; a three-day meeting.

Independently of all this, I was trying to pursue my career in the fire service. In 1991 applications were called to attend a course conducted by the CHEM unit. This organisation was designed to instruct all emergency services about the proper procedures and coordination required in the event of any sort of emergency involving chemicals. The names of applicants were assessed by a senior officer called Dick Hart. I was excluded from the course. I called Dick Hart and asked him what reference he made to my name on the list if any. He told me he had marked me as highly desirable. Somebody had interfered with the list and ruled me out.

I contacted the Human Rights and Equal Opportunity Commission and made a complaint explaining the matter fully. They investigated on my behalf and found that I had indeed been excluded without reason. The end result of their work was an invitation to attend the next course in 1991 and a letter from Commissioner Belcher confirming that I would not be discriminated against on the basis of my trade union activity. If only those who had followed Commissioner Belcher respected and maintained his promise.

There was a big surprise waiting for me in this course. The officer co-ordinating the course, Greg Adams, approached me and told me that I was to be the presenter to the class for the fire service. I said, "but I'm a student, a member of the class." He said, "I have been told that you are the best man we have in the fire service to make these presentations". When it was time for fire service presentations, I got out of my students chair, went to the front of the class, and adopted a lecturer's persona; The Fire Service Act, the role of the fire service at an incident, et cetera.

Some qualifications including advanced resuscitation, high angle rescue, and road accident rescue.

Some more qualifications including certificate IV, hazardous management from QUT, fire investigation, and an appreciation from the police force.

After which I resumed my chair as a student member of the class. Fire service officers in the class included at least one senior officer.

Chapter 4. Amalgamation.

SOME TIME IN 1986 – 87 it was proposed that the three firefighters unions—the UFU, the MFBOA and the Country Fire Officers Association—should consider amalgamation. There was much discussion among the members, and ultimately it was decided to hold a ballot among the membership to decide the issue. I did not believe that the membership would decide in favour of amalgamation. Nevertheless, I have always been a strong believer in the democratic process and I believed the membership should make the decision. When the ballot was conducted, the surprising result was that the overwhelming majority voted in favour of amalgamation. This meant that the three unions would become one, i.e. the Country Fire Officers Association and the MFBOA would cease to exist. These were dramatic changes. It meant that we would now all reconvene in the fireman's messroom for union meetings. It meant that these meetings would be chaired by Bruce Robertson, the current state president of the UFU and chair of the Brisbane branch. Some of these meetings were volatile. It was obvious that the two separate ranks had different needs, different concerns, but the officers were outnumbered and struggled to be heard, especially by Bruce Robertson.

One of the issues he really didn't care about was the difference in working hours between officers and firemen. Firemen had a Z shift to repay them for the extra two hours per week above the award 40 hours. Officers were not compensated at all. It meant that officers were working two hours a week for nothing. This was brought up for discussion on many occasions at Brisbane branch meetings but Bruce Robertson didn't want to know about it.

Another issue that he avoided was the issue of firemen's axes. Brisbane was the only fire service in Queensland issued with a fireman's axe carried on a belt. The new Queensland Fire Service was not going to issue axes in the future, despite almost every firefighter of every rank in Brisbane wanting to keep them. He told the meetings that air circulation under the turnout coat was necessary and a belt would restrict this. When it was pointed out that at any major structural fire we wore breathing apparatus with straps vertical and horizontal, making any air circulation under the turnout coat impossible; he was unmoved. The basic reason for this (from the Queensland Fire Service) was cost. The Brisbane Fire Service was really the only completely professional Fire Brigade in Queensland. Fire Brigades at that time were ranked according to their professional standards and ability to respond. All brigades were categorised in this way giving them a personal ranking of AAA, AA, A, B, et cetera. Brisbane was the only Triple-A brigade in Queensland. Among many differences, it was the only Fire Brigade issued with personal fireman's axes. The bureaucrats had a simple choice: – issue axes to the rest of the state with training or remove Brisbane's axes. The second option saved them an awful lot of money. Bruce Robertson was ignoring the directions he received at the branch and supporting the government's choice. I have never been to a structural fire where I did not find my axe extremely useful. Every man on my shift at Roma Street continued to wear their old turnout coats until they retired despite being issued with the new coats. When I retired I had to hand in a list of personal equipment. On the list was my axe. I told Gary little, who was receiving my equipment, that I was keeping it. He understood, he said that's fine. Also on the list was my new turnout clothing. I handed that in unworn.

Bruce Robertson did not keep the chair long. During my management of the MFBOA I had rung Bruce Robertson's home number to discuss certain matters. His wife answered the phone and said, "he's not here anymore, call the union office". About this time, the UFU had hired a research officer named Dinah Priestley. What he did with his personal life was really none of my affair; it became my concern when the new research officer had too much control over the union business. On one occasion at an evening union meeting, Bruce Robertson arrived with Dinah Priestley to attend the meeting. The members in attendance immediately demanded that Dinah Priestley leave, not being a member of the union. It was put to a vote, and almost unanimously Priestley was ordered to leave. Robertson immediately declared that he did not want to attend the meeting anymore and followed Priestley out the door. Shortly after at another meeting the change in chairmanship was formalised and I was elected as chair of the Brisbane branch.

On one day when I returned home my wife told me she had a phone call from a man claiming to be an interstate truck driver. He told her I was having a sexual relationship with his wife when he was not home. She had the presence of mind to delay him while she got a tape recorder. He then gained more confidence and told her I was also "playing up" with his mate's wife as well. She told me he lost her at that point, she said I just wasn't that good. Apparently my wife didn't believe I would be able to satisfy three women at the same time. When it became apparent he had not established any matrimonial disharmony, he rang again and told my wife "he's fuckin' dead!" I took these taped messages to the next Brisbane branch meeting of the UFU and played them to the meeting. I then said, bluntly, "I want this man. Does anybody know who this is? Can anyone identify this voice?" There was silence. The man who was responsible for the phone calls may have been present at the meeting, but nobody was able or willing to give me any clues.

Resolutions from the Brisbane branch were duly taken to regular meetings of the State Committee of Management of the UFU. I was one of the delegates with this responsibility. Any resolutions from the Brisbane branch were directed to the state secretary, Stephen Robertson, who incidentally was not a firefighter but a political appointment. These meetings were a farce. Brisbane branch's resolutions were always the last on the agenda and we always ran out of time, meaning that Brisbane's concerns were never raised. At the time, the Brisbane branch had over 40% of the membership of the union, but at the SCM meetings, we had approximately 10% of the vote. It was the worst gerrymander in the history of Australia.

Some of the officers expressed concern about the numbers in the amalgamation ballot; it seemed that quite a number had voted no in the amalgamation vote. They began to push for an investigation into the whole affair. This resulted in a commission of enquiry chaired by Commissioner Cooke. Some time in 1989 I received a phone call from Alan Mcsporen, counsel assisting Commissioner Cooke. He asked me if I would become a witness in the enquiry. I told him I had a problem with that. He said, "what your problem?" I told him that whatever the men did when conducting the ballot, they were fire officers, they were family men, and I did not want to see them penalised. He advised me that there was no law in existence concerning amalgamation ballots, so whatever the decision of the enquiry, no charges would be laid. I told him under those circumstances I would be a witness. Commissioner Cooke decided at the end of the inquiry that the amalgamation ballot was "fraudulently rigged". He confirmed my earlier advice that no charges would be laid. He also declared that he was not able to, in his words, unscramble the egg, so the fraudulently constructed UFU would remain.

I continued to attend State committee of management meetings, trying to put forward Brisbane branch resolutions, mostly without much success. Stephen Robertson had been elected to parliament as reward for his services to his party, and had been obliged to resign from his position as secretary of the UFU. On one such meeting, I noticed that Dinah Priestley seemed to be conducting the meeting. It took a while for this behaviour to register, because she always was in attendance at these meetings, beside Bruce Robertson's elbow, but it now seemed to me that she was much more dominant. Eventually it became apparent that she had been appointed as union secretary. I made a decision then that I could not tolerate this, and when I left the meeting I sought other options. I had previously had suspicions about her status in the union, but union membership lists were closely guarded and not available to membership. When I ran for office I called the state returning officer, declared myself as a candidate in the coming union election, and asked for a copy of the union membership. He willingly complied. There on the list of members was Dinah Priestley, listed as an active fireman in Brisbane. This was done without the knowledge of the rank and file, but her appointment as union secretary was a step too far.

My defection.

I approached Bill Ludwig, gained his support, and began recruiting members. I held an AWU meeting at Kemp Place fire station, the first of its kind in many years. It was well attended. I offered the attendees the opportunity to resign from the UFU and join up. We gained many members on the night and continued to steadily increase our membership. Priestley decided to make an application to the Industrial Commission to give the UFU exclusive rights. Despite the fact that the UFU was losing members to the AWU, despite the fact that the AWU already had members long-term in the fire service, the Industrial Commission gave her exclusive access. The circumstances in plain and simple terms were as follows: – Robertson and Priestley had lost support of the Brisbane branch of the UFU, their membership in Brisbane was bleeding towards the AWU, the AWU was actively supporting firefighters in Brisbane, and yet through the support of the Industrial Commission, Robertson and Priestley gained exclusive rights.

Regional Commander Alan Bartlett immediately banned me from holding any AWU meetings at Kemp Place. I told him we would assemble at Kemp Place and walk to the AWU building. He didn't like that but didn't think he could do anything about it. We had not lost our AWU membership, but we could not recruit any more and the AWU could not negotiate on our behalf with the management of the fire service or the Industrial Commission. We formed an association titled the Queensland Democratic Firefighters Association Inc. It was registered as an incorporated body. It meant that we could meet, make decisions, and correspond. This clearly was out of favour with the bureaucrats. On one occasion, because I wrote to Commissioner Jeff Skerritt about what we saw as important issues, Commissioner Skerritt communicated with Alan Bartlett instructing him to book me in for formal counselling for daring to send him such a communication. We had to make a change, so we made my wife honorary secretary by unanimous vote, after which all correspondence would be signed by her. I was confident that she would not be booked in for formal counselling, and if they were foolish enough to do that, they would probably have a hard time. Eventually, with the passage of time and the change of personnel in key positions we were able to cancel the incorporation of our association in 1996, but it had served us well.

My belief in trade unions and their operation has never varied. I've always believed that trade unions are a great thing, whether it is the United Firefighters Union or the Cattlemen's Union. Such unions exist and function for the safeguard and benefit of their members, and for the service they provide to the community. If you are elected to a position in a trade union, you are a servant of the membership. You do not owe any allegiance to any political party. If you disagree with the wishes of the membership, you can discuss, attempt to persuade, or argue, but ultimately if you cannot agree with the wishes of the membership you should resign.

If you are elected to represent members of the union, you have an obligation to meet, discuss, and negotiate matters with the elected members of parliament no matter what party they belong to.

After the UFU gained exclusive access to the fire service, I made an application to rejoin. It was rejected. Over a period of time, I made a number of applications, all of which were rejected. I Contacted Henry Lawrence, who was running the union at that time, and told him I wanted a meeting with him and the State committee of Management. He set a date. On the day of this meeting, I asked these assembled men what it was that gave them grounds to reject my application for union membership. There was some comment and interchange between us, but really there was no reason. I advised them before I left the meeting that if I could not achieve membership I would seek a legal solution. One of them said, "that sounds like a threat." I said, "no it's not a threat, I simply think you should know what might happen next before you make a decision".

That was in fact the process we had to follow. I engaged Con Sciacca, a man who believed in everybody's right to belong to a union. Very quickly, the attitude from the union changed. The state committee of Management passed a resolution inviting me to join the union, which of course I did. I maintained this membership until my retirement.

After my retirement, where your membership is terminated because you are no longer an active firefighter, I became a member of the Retired Firefighters Association. In their regular circular, they advise that union membership is available to retired firefighters. This is not strictly true, it only applies if the union management likes you. I had applied for membership as a retired firefighter but it had always been rejected.

Chapter 5. Victimisation, discrimination and harassment.

THE SORT OF STUFF THAT GOES UNDER THE HEADINGS in this chapter has no place in an organisation like the fire service. These things would not have occurred in the Brisbane Metropolitan Fire Brigade. Unfortunately, occurrences of this type of behaviour were frequent.

In 1993 I was requested by Wayne Hartley to attend new recruits at Lytton training centre as an AWU union representative. I was contacted by Alan Musk to arrange a day and a time. I offered to go down in my own time on any day that I was not rostered on duty. Musk insisted there was only one day I could attend, a day shift that I was rostered on; he would not move on that date. Unperturbed, I agreed. It was not difficult for a station officer at Roma Street to travel in a turntable ladder (the vehicle that was my responsibility) to another Fire Brigade destination. On the day in question, I summoned my crew to the ladder, booked out of the station on radio and proceeded towards Lytton. I recieved a radio message telling me to call into the nearest fire station and telephone superintendent George Malouf. I did so, and he told me I could not take the ladder to Lytton. I protested, telling him I had been asked to do so and that arrangements had been made, but he was unrepentant and told me I'd have to make other arrangements. I booked the ladder off duty and made my way to Lytton, where I was able in the presence of David Darcy from the AWU to address the new recruits. Separated from my fire appliance, I booked off sick for the rest of the day, a matter of hours.

On my next day on at Roma Street Station I was told by Peter George that I was not to leave the station without his specific permission. This meant of course, that I could not really carry out my duties as station officer at Roma Street. Soon after I was served with charges about this particular matter which was supposed to be investigated and heard by regional Commander Alan Bartlett, whom I suspect was the instigator of the whole episode. Bartlett interviewed me and then wanted to talk to my crew. I said yes fine, but I am their union rep and I will stay with them. He didn't expect that, clearly it left him with a dilemma. It was probably his intention to cajole, threaten, or intimidate my crew into saying whatever would support the attack against me. He could not do that while I was sitting there in front of him. There was a set time frame for him to deliver his decision after which I would be allowed a certain amount of time to appeal the decision that I already knew he would make. The delivery of his decision was a couple of weeks late, in fact I had to call him more than once asking him to deliver.

In the meantime, I received a phone call asking me to volunteer to go down to New South Wales because of the bushfires that were out of control and their requests for help. I was on leave, so I said yes I will go. We were to be taken down to New South Wales in a coach along with the usual firefighting equipment and clothing. Bartlett delivered his very predictable decision to me at Kemp Place as I was about to climb on the bus. I warned him that I would need the two weeks preparation for appeal starting from when I returned from New South Wales. He had no option but to agree. I travelled down to the fireground in NSW with Bartlett's determination in my pocket.

The appeals hearing was chaired by Brian Walsh, former Brisbane Lord Mayor, who had been appointed Appeals Commissioner. Bartlett relied on two things; the evidence from Alan Musk and George Malouf. Musk simply testified that he had seen me arrive at Lytton in a turntable ladder. In hindsight, it is now obvious to me that Alan Musk was the linchpin in this whole saga. It took me completely by surprise. I had known Alan Musk since he joined the fire service, in fact I had been his training officer when he was on probation. His father, Gordon, was an old workmate and long-term friend. If you had to pick somebody to set this up that would not arouse my suspicions, Alan Musk was the perfect choice.

I was given information from a number of sources about an officer's course at Lytton that Alan Musk ran. On the last day of the course, he sent a Fire Brigade utility with a driver down to the Pinkenba hotel to buy a carton of beer, which he shared with the course members. I was given the name of the driver, and the registration number of the utility. I was also given a list of the names of the officers who attended the course. This evidence under examination would have destroyed Alan Musk and his reputation. It would also have damaged a lot of other officers, and it would have done serious damage to his father, Gordon. He was his father's only son. There had to be another way.

George Malouf, under oath, testified that the fire service had four pieces of aerial equipment and they had to be kept in the city at all times. This was not true. Aerial equipment has often been sent with its officer and crew to a number of places as requested by the fire service. In fact, I have seen two turntable ladders extended to make a big arch at Lytton training centre on the day that probationers graduated.

I had given Commissioner Walsh a statement by regional Commander Keith Drummond that he wished to give evidence. Keith Drummond was the last chief officer of Brisbane, the most experienced senior officer in Queensland, and second in rank only to the Commissioner. Keith Drummond would have told the hearing that Malouf's statement was completely false. The trouble was, there was no facility in the appeals process that allowed me to subpoena anybody. Anybody who was going to give evidence had to be virtually invited to do so. Bartlett was certainly not going to give Keith Drummond such an invitation. I believe on the day that he might have appeared, he was given some project that sent him out of the office. On the second day of the hearing, Commissioner Walsh made it quite obvious that he wanted to wrap it up on that day. In fact, it appeared to me that he wanted to go early. He made some references to the Irish club, there must've been something big on at the club that day, and I think he could taste his 1st pint of Guinness.

We needed some time to gain an extra day so that we could arrange for Keith Drummond to give evidence. Assisting Alan Bartlett was a man called Tim Davey, a minor bureaucrat. We approached Tim Davey and spent some time in negotiation until finally we told him we were going to make a deal. We had no such intention of doing so. What should have happened next was that Tim Davey should have requested a meeting with Commissioner Walsh and us in camera. At that point, we would have said, no he is mistaken, we made no such agreement, and we wish to continue with the hearing. At that point, looking at the clock and mindful that he was already late to attend the Irish club, Commissioner Walsh would have no choice but to give us another day.

Unfortunately, Tim Davey wrecked the whole plan unintentionally. He stood up and told the hearing that we did not have to proceed any further, we had made a deal. Commissioner Walsh had to advise him that he had just prejudiced the entire hearing, and we could not proceed any further. The further problem for Commissioner Walsh was that he himself could not take any further action in this hearing, and another Commissioner or Deputy Commissioner had never been appointed. He adjourned untill the following working day.

On that day, he decided to deliver a compromise. I believe he was probably advised to uphold the original penalty imposed by Bartlett, which was to reduce me down to the fireman's ranks for 12 months. Without giving me further opportunity to carry on my appeal, he could not do that, but he probably had instructions from a much higher level that he could not dismiss the charges.

What he delivered was half of everything that Bartlett had imposed. I was reduced by one rank but still an officer, and only for six months. The whole thing was a disgraceful charade designed to destroy any influence I had on the rank and file. I believe it is a testimony to my self-control that none of the people who appeared to bring me down were injured or killed. The one other interesting feature about this episode happened when we were in New South Wales dealing with the fire hazard. I had a crew and equipment to carry out hazard reduction and fire protection in a certain area, and one of the men in my crew was Peter George, George Malouf's offsider and the same man who ordered me at Roma Street not to go anywhere without his specific permission. I can say on this occasion that he carried out orders and was a useful member of the crew.

Immediately after this shambles, I was issued with new epaulets carrying the reduced officer markings. By the time I received these, and I had returned from leave, winter was approaching. Officers were issued with a cardigan, and I chose to wear mine on a daily basis. On occasions when I was in Bartlett's office discussing Fire Brigade business, he would look at me and say, "aren't you hot?" I would reply, "no I'm fine". He wanted to see the new epaulets. He would have had to look in the plastic they came in because I never wore them. In fact, on the day that I handed in some of my equipment, I passed the two epaulets across the desk still in the wrapper and said, "send these back to Peter George".

On 5 March 1996 Malouf demonstrated to me how bad his testimony was. He asked to see me and told me to take the only aerial still operating in Brisbane at the time, to Bundamba. Apparently the workshops needed to change some elevated exterior lights at the fire station. I looked at him and said, "this is the only aerial still operating in Brisbane at the moment." He replied, "yes, I know." His eyes remained focused on his desk. He would not look at me. I left Roma Street Station at 08:30 hours and after Bundamba I was sent on to Karana Downs. I arrived back at Roma Street Station after midday.

I have one more example of the hypocrisy of George Malouf's testimony about keeping all of our aerial equipment in the city. On 14 November 1995 I was contacted by the duty officer at Kemp Place to tell me that a turntable ladder was required at Lytton training centre by 10:30 hours for an aerial demonstration. When I arrived at Lytton I discovered that this display was for the benefit of seven children and seven adults making up a preschool playgroup. At the time, this turntable ladder was the only one available in Brisbane. I reported this incident and all its details to Peter George, who was an assistant district commander at the time.

This was just the first of many examples of victimisation and discrimination. In 1995 I was required to attend a hearing at the Industrial Relations Commission as a witness for the AWU. It was a day that I was normally rostered on duty. I found another officer on another shift that I could swap with so that I would be off duty to appear. It was not an uncommon practice to arrange such swaps, and it was within the authority of the duty officer to do so, and I was that duty officer. Before I arranged the swap, Malouf had ordered me to go to Dutton Park police station to carry out a lecture as a JEST course instructor. When he found out the day before that I had arranged the swap, he raced over to the roster office looking for some confirmation there of the swap. It had nothing to do with the roster office and was not their responsibility, but Malouf didn't seem to know that, or wanted at least to pretend that he didn't know that. He called me and ordered me to attend work the next day and go to the police station as he had originally ordered me to do. I called the AWU office and told them of my problem. They told me to go to work, attend the police station, and they would take care of it. I did exactly that, was partway through my address to a collection of police officers, when another officer came through the door and told me that he would finish the instruction, gave me a set of keys, and told me I was to return to Roma Street Station. When I got there, Malouf appeared very embarrassed and arranged for me to be transported down to the Industrial Relations Commission. I was told later that Bill Ludwig telephoned Bartlett and told him if he needed to he could subpoena me to appear, but if he did have to do that he would subpoena Bartlett and Malouf as well. That might be why I was suddenly relieved at the police station.

Nevertheless, these wonderful senior officers I had to deal with saw another opportunity, and I was charged with anything they could think of to do with changing rosters and shift attendance. They had a problem of course. The political landscape was changing and the existing government was worried that it could get tossed out. All members of parliament and all bureaucrats were prepared to do anything at all that might keep their arses in the chairs of power.

I had organised a firemen's march through the city to Parliament house. It was basically because of the complete contempt of manning levels in Brisbane. The operational fire staff shifts did not carry any extras; as it stood if anybody was off sick they were not replaced and if we had a number off sick we dropped an appliance off the run. Obviously, if we had a lot of sick on one day, this could lead to pumps off the run and even stations closed. This was not the case outside of Brisbane. In country centres, if they needed to, they would call a man in to replaced the sick. For their annual income, rank and file firemen in country centres were making more money than station officers in Brisbane.

After all preparations and every effort was made to make sure we would have a successful march, I still had this nagging fear in my gut. Even if we did everything, arranged everything, what if nobody came? I need not have worried, they turned up by the hundreds.

When we got to Parliament house, I saw a lot of angry men. The minister at the time, Tom Burns, come out to address the men and made a fool of himself. He was in fact insulting and offensive. I looked at a lot of angry faces and I thought I might have even had to intervene to protect him from harm, but that was not the case. These were angry firemen but they would not do something like that. We made every TV channel that night and the front page of the Courier Mail the next day. In spite of all that, Burns decided to dig in. At the next Brisbane branch meeting, everybody wanted to know what we would do next. I should add that while I attended these meetings at the messroom at Kemp Place I was not a member of the UFU, having been denied membership.

After the Industrial Commission gave exclusive access to the fire service to the UFU, I had made several applications for membership, each application being rejected. I even have one letter from Scott Morgan, a station officer from Southport who was acting secretary at the time, telling me I had been rejected because I was of general 'bad character'.

The meeting would go ahead and from time to time they would ask my advice. They wanted another march, but I advised them it would simply be a repeat and it would not attract much attention. They said what can we do to draw more attention, and I replied it might be good if we could get three services in the march. They said can you do that? I said give me a few days. I contacted the president of the police union and asked could we get any police attendance at a march? He said I can get you some but not many. I said that's fine as long as we have the uniform present. I then tried the ambulance and they were willing to take part. I passed this on to the Brisbane branch and they were ready to go. Burns got to know about it and immediately saw a political disaster and caved in, giving Brisbane callbacks like the rest of the state. The interesting thing is, the man I was dealing with in the ambulance was also named Wilkinson, no relation, but I think Burns thought it was a family conspiracy.

Rob Borbidge came out to address the firefighters and was greeted with cheers and applause. The bureaucrats in office saw this as very ominous.

During Tom Burns' address to the firefighters, he said, "there will be no get squares." I said to him, "that's already happening." He said, "write to me, tell me about it". So of course I did, including all the details of fabricated charges and restrictions. Suddenly everything changed. I received a visit at Roma Street Station from Mike Hall, a man who had received rapid promotion to the senior ranks. Mike Hall began his career as a fireman at Pine Rivers Fire Brigade. Promotions in brigades like that were at the whim of the chief officer; no exams needed. These officers became known in Brisbane as "Pine Rivers subbies". Mike Hall was the quintessential Pine Rivers subbie, which means he now had a senior position in the Queensland Fire Service without having ever having sat for an officer's exam. We had coffee and an agreeable conversation in the officer's messroom upstairs. He told me that all charges were dropped and the Director-General, Leo Keliher, would like to have a meeting with me. After a couple of cancellations we finally had the meeting in Keliher's office at Forbes house, what was then Fire Service headquarters, with Commissioner Jeff Skerritt.

During the conversation, an agreeable one, Keliher assured me that all attacks on me would cease. He then said, "we have become aware that you have some influence in the fire service. We are in a bit of trouble and we'd like your help". This was truly remarkable. The kingpin of the attacks against me suddenly wanted my help. I waited for what should have followed in his conversation; something like, we do apologise for the unwarranted attacks against you, we realise you've been ignored and stepped over when it comes to promotion, and we intend to make that up. I waited. Nothing more. I looked at him and said, "Leo, I'll do whatever I can."

At the next election, we had a change of government and Leo was moved out. I believe he might have gained a position under the New South Wales government, which was then held by his party. I even received a letter from Commissioner Skerritt confirming that I would not, in the future, be discriminated against. This was the second such assurance I had received from the boss of the fire service; unfortunately, there were senior officers in the service who did not abide by these assurances.

There is one other interesting character involved in the to-ing and fro-ing of union business. While stationed at Roma Street, I heard about a man who seemed to have some position in the fire service management; Brendan McKennariey. I phoned fire service headquarters asking to speak to this man. I was told they had no record of anybody by that name holding any position in the fire service. Shortly after, someone rang me back saying Mr Mckennariey did not hold any position, but he visited frequently to talk to different people. Later on the same day, I received a telephone call from Brendan inviting me to lunch at the Eatons Hill Hotel. It was convivial, it was a long lunch. During the course of the lunch, among other advice, he told me he was a card-carrying member of the Labour Party.

Much later, when state elections were looming, I received a call from the President of the Police Union. He had received a call from a petty criminal that he had knowledge of telling him that McKennariey wanted to have a meeting with me. Why did he not call me directly? Why did he use a third-party to call the Police Union (PU)? These questions remained unanswered. I decided to go to his house and protect myself with a tape recorder. Basically, Brendan's concerns revolved around the coming election. He did not know what actions I might take, if any, and he was obviously fishing for clues. He then approached the subject of my exclusion from the United Firefighters union, telling me that he could arrange for my application for membership to be accepted, if I agreed not to run for office. It was a fairly lengthy discussion, but that was the essence of it. I made no promises. He then asked for a meeting with the President of the Police Union. I told him I would pass his message on, but I coud give no assurances.

When I told the PU president, he said what does he want to talk to me for? We talked about it, and agreed to let him have the meeting, but he would, like me, protect himself by recording the conversation. Once again, Brendan's concerns revolved around the election, he said I was considered a loose cannon and nobody knew what I might do. He said that he was looking for someone who might have some influence on what I would or would not do. The reply was that no-one could not control what I did, but in any case, what's in it for him? Brendan replied that there were some new senior rank applications coming up and he would write my application for me. I have never been a party to those sorts of deals.

The list of discriminations against me is extensive, and I will list here the ones I know about.

On 4 October 1994 Peter George was sick. Kevin Brazel, a station officer working with me in the duty office, was moved upstairs to act as the senior officer. This was George Malouf's decision.

On 5 October Peter George was still sick but now it gets a little more complicated because Kevin Brazel is also sick. There was an attempt to move Alan Nunan from Kemp Place to Roma Street to take up the acting position, but he refused to go, simply saying it wasn't right. I was then moved upstairs in the acting position because all other avenues had been exhausted.

On 10 October 1994 Peter George was transferred to Petrie. Kevin Brazel was moved upstairs to act as a senior officer for six weeks.

In 1995 I contacted Forbes house, Fire service headquarters at the time, and made arrangements to see my personal file. When I got there, it was missing and nobody knew where it was. Communication from me seeking some explanation brought a letter from Commissioner Skerritt apologising for the missing file and assuring me that every effort would be made to find it. I wondered if it really was missing or if there was material in it that nobody wanted me to see.

In 1997 the Area Director at Roma Street was Kerry Tupper and I was the duty officer downstairs. I knew that Tupper would soon be going on leave and I told him I would like the opportunity to act in his place upstairs. He said yeah fine. On my first day on after his leave commenced, I found John Van Klaveren acting in Tupper's place. I did some detective work. I found that Van Klaveren had been in a day job at Forbes house, Area Director Ian Gilbert had been moved from Wynum to Forbes house and a station officer had been moved to act in Gilbert's place at Wynnum. When he returned from leave, I asked Tupper what happened. He said, "Peter George overruled my recommendation".

In 1997 I was stationed at Nundah fire station when the Area Director Kevin Foster was moved to the city on a long-term project. I was the obvious choice to replace him, but another station officer, Ross Watts, was moved from Kemp Place to take up the position.

I asked Kevin Foster who made the choice, and he said, "Peter George".

From the 17th to 21 November 1997 Area Director Ian Gilbert was absent from his position. I was downstairs. No appointments were made. For that week, the office remain closed and Roma Street did not have an Area Director.

In 1998 I was stationed at Caboolture fire station, and the Area Director was Kerry Tupper. He was about to go on leave, and I wondered what would happen this time. Tupper left his recommendation to the last possible minute, nominating me as his replacement. This time, Peter George would not have enough time to change it, so I served my time as an actor. During my stay in this capacity I achieved two things: –

1. The rates from the Caboolture Shire Council came into my office for the fire station. The bill was large because a fire station uses a lot of water through necessity and the station was being billed as if it was a private house. I contacted the Shire Council, explained to them that the needs of a fire station are considerably different to a private residence and convinced them that we should be billed at a much cheaper rate.
2. This involves a visit from the minister, Merri Rose. I had the opportunity to escort her around the station explaining all of the equipment and what it did. I noticed when her driver was trying to enter the station from King Street (the main street) he had a long wait. In conversation with the Minister, I commented on this and said it would be useful if we had some remote control over the traffic lights. She replied in the affirmative. The next day I contacted the appropriate bureaucrat and requested traffic lights that could be controlled by the fire station. He said that I could apply in writing but he didn't think I would be successful. I said to him, "the minister was here at the station yesterday and she has requested them. If I can't get them I have to report to her, what was your name?" We had the traffic lights in a fortnight.

When Peter George wrote a formal approval to Kerry Tupper for my acting appointment, he asked Tupper for a performance report while I was his replacement. Peter George's timing was bad. When he sent the letter asking for a performance report I was in Tupper's office already acting. I shared it with Tupper when he returned, commenting I'd never seen such a request before, he replied neither have I. There were also some questions about the installation of the traffic lights; it was suggested that I should have conferred with the ambulance before I got the job done (Caboolture is a station combining both fire and ambulance). Tupper replied that he had been working on this project (the traffic lights) for some time and it was not a new proposition to the ambulance. He also advised, in writing, that my performance in the acting position was "very satisfactory". Such a request for a written performance report had never happened before and probably will never happen again, so I was the only station officer with a positive written report about my performance. One would think this would mean that I would be first cab off the rank for any future acting positions. On the contrary, I never received another.

In 1998, still at Caboolture, there was an opportunity for another acting position in the Area Director's office. I was still stationed there, with my positive performance report. The acting position was filled by Tom Denson.

I want to make it clear that I have no criticism of the officers who were given the opportunity to fill these actor ranks, on the contrary, I'm glad they had this opportunity.

There were other examples of acting positions where I was purposely excluded, but the ones I have listed here make it obvious that Peter George was carrying out Alan Bartlett's illegal orders. I was advised by senior officers that Alan Bartlett had given an instruction that Bruce Wilkinson was not to be given any acting positions because of his union activity. This instruction of course is a violation of the Anti-discrimination Act and the Industrial Relations Act. Nevertheless, some officers faithfully carried it out.

I have in my possession a statement signed by Shane Barker on the 14th of the 12th 2002. Shane Barker was a fire officer who had been with the service for 16 years and a station officer for seven years. He states that he attended a birthday party in 1994 for Jock

Honeyman. One of the people in attendance was Peter George. According to the statement, Peter George said, "you're not involved in that union shit of Wilkie's are you? He's got no chance of a senior rank, he's a marked man. He wants to act upstairs, and yet he carries on like this." The statement further refers to a memorial service at St Brigid's Church in 2001 where similar comments were made, Peter George extended his hand, and Barker turned away.

I learned I had to be careful about what I said and to whom, even if it was a joke. As the duty officer at Roma Street, I would communicate with the duty officer at Kemp Place at the start of every shift, making note of any absentees and other matters that might be important for the running of the service on that day. On a particular day in 1994 I was communicating with the duty officer at Kemp Place, Peter Fraser, on such matters. In taking note of any men off sick, Peter advised me that Bruce Robertson was off sick. I said as a joke," may be he is cutting out his sick pay. "Peter replied, "I'll ask him." This was not unusual humorous banter between duty officers on any day.

The problem was, Peter Fraser actually did ask him. Bruce Robertson, the man I had replaced as chair of the Brisbane branch of the union, obviously saw this as an opportunity and made a complaint to Alan Bartlett. Bartlett carried out an investigation, asking me if I had said such things, and of course I replied, no I don't know what you're talking about. Peter Fraser when asked said I did, but without any corroborating evidence for this terrible crime, he could go no further and the matter was dropped. Robertson could not accept this. Ignoring all the rank structure in existence, he wrote directly to the Director-General, Leo Keliher, who was probably a mate from the same political faction. Keliher immediately communicated with the Commissioner, Jeff Skerritt. His hand written note reads as follows: –" Jeff, please brief me on progress made in this matter. I am disturbed by the apparently continual role of Mr Wilkinson in the activities of the Q FS – primarily a disruptive role." Of course, they had to get back to Leo telling him there was no evidence to support Robertson's complaint, but they assured him that they would keep the file open. Considering how serious this matter was, I can understand that.

After all of these numerous attacks, it become apparent to me that I would not always be able to survive. I needed a plan B in case the fabricated charges and allegations became serious enough to threaten my existence. I found a man who was qualified as both a lawyer and a psychiatrist. I booked myself in for counselling in 1995. If I needed qualified support, this professional would be it. The information I gave him about harassment and persecution by the management was no surprise to him. He had seen examples of it in the police force.

Chapter 6. Other innocent victims.

ON SEVERAL OCCASIONS I WAS CONTACTED BY OTHER FIREMEN who were threatened by the bureaucracy or dubious senior officers. I had a phone call on one occasion from Alan Verrall, a fireman who had served in my crew at Taigum fire station. He was on leave, and related an incident to me seeking my advice. He had been doing some work at his house and had some sort of accident leaving him unconscious. His girlfriend found him and took him to the Redcliffe Hospital for treatment. He remained unconscious through all of this and remembers nothing. Apparently, he must have said something which offended the doctor who was treating him. I have been told that this is not unusual with unconscious patients. He had received advice from his area director, Ian Gilbert at Roma Street, that he had received a complaint from the doctor that had to be dealt with. Ian Gilbert had passed it on to Peter George, who was now Regional Commander stationed at fire service headquarters at Kedron Park. Even though he was on leave, he was proposing to go in to Kedron Park and finish up this matter. Alarm bells started to ring in my head. I said, "you're not going on your own are you?" He said, "well yes, I was just gonna go in and finish it all up." I said, "you should not go on your own." He said, "well, what are you doing on that day?"

When we got to Peter George's office, he was aggressive and threw a report block at Verrall and invited him to write out his resignation. If Verrall had picked up the pen I think I might have broken his fingers. He did not. Ian Gilbert was present, sitting behind us in the corner. There was a constant barrage of negative material from Peter George, but Verrall held his ground. In the midst of this, I said to Peter George "you understand he was unconscious don't you?" He said, "yes I know that." After some time, I said to Peter George, "are we done?" He said, "yes were done." Verrall and I moved downstairs to the car park and said to him," When you get home I want you to immediately write down as much of this interview as you can remember. When you get to work at Roma Street, go upstairs to Ian Gilbert's office and ask him for a copy of the doctor's complaint. If you don't immediately get it, ask him every day until you do." He told me later that Gilbert finally confessed that there was no written complaint, only a phone call. The doctor, in making that phone call to the employer of his patient complaining about his patient's behaviour, who happened to be unconscious, committed a gross violation of the doctor's ethics, and could have been the subject of a complaint to the Australian medical Association. In any case, Gilbert should have recognised it for what it was, pacified the doctor, and left the matter behind him. It should never have been a matter to discuss in Peter George's office.

I saw Alan Verrall much later at a hardware store. He was out of the service. They found something else to use as a tool to terminate his employment.

Another example refers to the prosecution of a station officer who shall remain nameless because he may still be employed. At the very start of this century, there was a high level of fire danger in the middle of a drought as we so often see in this country. A total fire ban had been applied. The station officer, giving due consideration to the risks in his area of responsibility, identified substantial dry growth which would, if ignited, pose a serious threat to nearby buildings. When conditions were right, he undertook a process known to fire officers as hazard reduction. This means basically, carefull burning of the dry growth under controlled conditions so that no damage is done. He carried out this exercise successfully without any damage to any structure. He was charged in the fire service by two senior officers for carrying out this operation during a total fire ban. Eventually, the man was prosecuted in the District Court. He had contacted me over this matter, and I advised him that I would make a statement in support and if necessary appear as a witness. I also found another experienced station officer who had served as a chief officer in a country brigade. This man also agreed to give evidence if necessary. The best way to demonstrate how ridiculous these charges were is to quote the judge.

His honour said, "it is presumed that Parliament, in enacting a law, does not produce an absurdity. What is contended for by the Crown does have that result. In this case, on the Crown argument, the applicant should have applied to himself, orally or in writing. As you are purporting to act under part six (that is, not for some routine purpose) he could have and presumably would have applied orally, that is talked to himself. He would have had to consider in his quasi-judicial capacity, the merits of his application, including, for example, whether he was telling himself the truth. And if he determined that he was failing to provide relevant information to himself or was telling himself lies, or attempting to mislead himself, penal sanctions would have been enlivened (section 147 (c)). The same consideration would apply had he taken the time and trouble to apply in writing." These remarks by the judge clearly show that his honour had a much better understanding of the Fire Service Act and the powers of an authorised fire officer than the fools who brought this diligent and conscientious fire officer to court. Needless to say, his honour threw the matter out.

In spite of this, within the fire service, the man was stripped of his officer rank and had to wait some years to reapply before he regained his position. It is absolutely disgraceful a conscientious fire officer should be treated this way by the very people who ought to defend him.

A firefighter who served with me at Roma Street was a man named Gary Walter, an exceptionally capable firefighter and a former police officer. Gary had decided to transfer to the Gold Coast fire service. He told me later he was subject to the usual harassment from the rank and file; they did not like boys from Brisbane. None of this would have any effect on him, he was too strong for anything they would throw at him.

On a particular day in about 2000, the training officer walked into their messroom and said, "you boys have all just past the necessary test to qualify you for a certificate IV. Okay? You will get them in the mail in due course." Gary was surprised at this, because he had not undertaken any steps to qualify him for this certificate. He had qualified for this certificate in Brisbane, so why would he want another one?

After giving it some thought, he believed he should report the matter to the senior officer, Bruce Byatt. Byatt reacted angrily, and Gary Walter said simply, "look, you do what you like with it, I'm simply telling you what's happening on your patch." Byatt replied that he'd have to have it in writing. Gary Walter, believing that he had been instructed to do so, wrote out a formal report on the matter. That simple process was the beginning of the end of Gary Walter's career in the fire service.

After a period of time, he received notification from Commissioner Hartley advising him that his employment was terminated. This is a man who did what he thought was right and it cost him his job. If he had simply kept his mouth shut and accepted the certificate like everybody else, he would have had no problems. He called me about it and brought all the correspondence to me; I addressed the matter with the police, but we really could not take any action. I said to him, "Why did you go to the gold coast? "He said, "Because I live there." He asked me later for a reference as he was seeking other employment; I gladly gave it. Some time later, the government had changed, Commissioner Hartley had gone, and I called him suggesting it might be possible for him to return if he wished. He had achieved a job in the mining sector and he said, "no thanks mate, I'm making more money than the Commissioner."

It was a great outcome in the long-term for him, but it was a loss for the fire service, losing a man for doing nothing more than the right thing.

Other phone calls.

I would often get calls, frequently at night, from firefighters who wanted to tell me something, who actually just wanted to talk to somebody about their trauma. One man rang me one night, someone I used to work with in my station, telling me about an incident that happened at a railway station on the western side of Brisbane. There had been a suicide; a man had decided to end it all by jumping in front of a train. The railways had cut off all power to the station and the line. The fire service was required to set up a lighting plant in the vicinity of the incident. The man who called me was on the train line when the lights came on. He looked down and saw the man's head at his feet. He was laughing a lot when he was talking to me but it was obvious to me that he did not think it was funny, it was just his way of dealing with it at the time. We talked for a while and he became calmer, and I told him to call me again if he'd like to.

I knew many men who suddenly displayed significant behavioural changes, due entirely to the things they had witnessed at an emergency. The incidents that have the most serious effect on firefighters are usually motor vehicle accidents (MVAs). Whenever there is an MVA it is attended by the fire service which has two responsibilities; to rescue anybody trapped in a vehicle and to neutralise any fire risk or other dangerous possibilities. People trapped in vehicle accidents can present a terrible sight; people with injuries to limbs, severe blood loss, people who have feet trapped under pedals, people whose upper body has impacted with the steering wheel, and any other possible injuries it is possible to think of. I have seen men, on their first encounter with such an incident, go pale and shaking. I have said to such men, "just go and sit down, take it easy, have some water." The impact of such images changes some men completely for life. They often retreat, initially from their immediate social circle, but ultimately from the community seeking refuge far removed from where they are. One man I know, who was a fairly loud, outgoing, comical character became completely the opposite. He eventually settled I am told in a small town on the Bass Strait Coast of Tasmania.

The images that you encounter in a motor vehicle accident stay with you all your life. I remember going to an accident on the Western Freeway, mid-morning. A young woman was obviously going out for a social encounter with friends. She was dressed up very nicely, she looked lovely, until you looked at her eyes, they were glassy, like the eyes you'd see in a doll. When you looked down just below the hem of her skirt her leg had received such damage it reminded you of meat you might see in a butcher shop. In the back seat of the car were a number of little fluffy toys, indicating that she probably had young children. That was many years ago, but I can still see that young woman in my head.

One night when I was stationed at Kenmore fire station, we were turned out to a motor vehicle accident in a suburban street not far from the station. In this case, a young man was driving a Monaro, V8 motor, four on the floor, and I believe he was probably not far from home when he collided with a large gumtree on the side of the road. His vehicle was almost torn in half. He was still strapped in with a full racing harness and he showed no external injuries at all even though he was unconscious. An ambulance officer was also in attendance and we were trying to administer oxygen to him when there was a terrible gurgling sound and blood poured out of his mouth. There was nothing we could do for him. Such encounters stay with you forever. It does affect you; you sleep badly for a while and you ponder sometimes whether there was anything you could have done that would make a difference in a particular incident. In my case, I have managed to deal with it; I have been lucky. Some friends of mine have not been so lucky and have paid a terrible price.

Chapter 7. The Terrible Tragedy.

IN 1994, A STRUCTURAL FIRE AT SOUTHPORT CLAIMED THE LIVES OF TWO FIREFIGHTERS. The structure was a two story brick house that was in use as a shop for bike repairs. This tragedy caused great consternation among the ranks, not only in Southport but right through the fire service.

I received a call from the office of Bill Potts, the lawyer, who was representing the widows of the two men. They told me they didn't understand Fire Brigade procedures and language, and they wanted some help. I asked them to give me a couple of days and I would call them back.

I put in a call to Commissioner Skerritt. I said to him, "Jeff this is terrible." He was, I believe, in shock. He had come from a small fire service in the Northern Territory and had never encountered anything like this before. I told him I wanted to help but I didn't know enough. He asked me what I needed and I said the information sheet from the communication centre would be a good start. He told me he would leave it at the front counter of his office, and I collected it from there. The information sheet on any incident records accurately every action, every communication from the fire ground to the communication centre and it is accurate to the minute. I then put in a call to Chris Adams at Channel 7 and asked him if they had any footage of the fire. He told me they had hours of it and I could come up and look at it.

What I saw on the screen was a shock. I saw a senior officer in shirtsleeves, no protective clothing, on a line of hose with a hose crew as if he was one of the fire crew. Beside the pump I saw the BA board (this is a board used to record any activity using breathing apparatus) containing the initials of the two men and what time they had begun using breathing apparatus. The information sheet told me that two senior officers had arrived at this incident and had been in attendance for some time before any thought was given to the two men. A senior officer, on arrival at a fire, must make himself aware of all of the detail involved in that fire, including how many fire staff he has and where they are. He should automatically check the BA board as soon as he arrives and take note of when any sets were put into use and when they are due to return.

What the information sheet told me was that the two men were probably dead about an hour before they were missed. I told Chris Adams to guard the film he had on the fire in case it went to court. He assured me he would lock it up.

I called Commissioner Skerritt again and told him I needed to look at the protective clothing the two men were wearing. He told me it was at Southport and he would call them and tell them I was coming to look at it. When I arrived at Southport Station, a senior officer came out and said, "we knew you were coming and we're not gonna tell you anything." I thought to myself, so much for the Commissioner's authority. I advised the Commissioner of this result and he told me he would get it moved to Beenleigh. The officer in charge at Beenleigh was Frank Sloman, formally from Brisbane, and I had no problem. Frank, the on-duty fire staff and I closely examined the protective clothing that the two men had been wearing. We agreed that it was obvious that this clothing have been worn in a fire but it had not failed, in fact it could still be worn again in combat.

I made a trip down to the office of Bill Potts and on the way I stopped to look at the fire scene. It was a two story brick house like many others you might see that had been used as a workshop. The fire was contained inside the building and the building was still standing and could possibly be renovated. The two men died approximately nine metres from the door, and they died simply because they ran out of air. I can say confidently that these two men would not have died if this fire had been in Brisbane. I took all of this information to Potts's office and explained the detail, proper practices, and terminology of the fire service. They became very confident about their case but they said to me they might need two witnesses, that is one more beside me. I made a phone call to Dave McIntosh, recently retired senior officer in charge of safety equipment in Brisbane, which managed anything to do with breathing apparatus. He exploded into the phone, "I'd charge those bastards" and I replied, "settle down Dave, the lawyers are looking for witnesses, will you appear?" He said yeah as long as I'm covered for expenses. I told him that would not be a problem.

We did not need to appear. The matter never went to court. The fire service paid the money rather than expose to the public eye the inadequacies and failures that appeared on that job.

There is one other legal matter worthy of mention. A Station officer friend of mine named Graham Jacobs who had retired called me to tell me he had terminal asbestosis. The nature of our profession frequently put us in close contact with asbestos in one form or another. Every pump carried a pair of asbestos gloves. On a given day, a member of the staff would be given the job of inspecting all of these and ticking them off on a worksheet. The man would go to the pump, take out the box containing the gloves, remove the gloves and shake off the dust, tick them off on the worksheet and move onto the next pump. At the fire ground, house fires frequently involved internal walls lined with asbestos material that were exploding and giving off clouds of dust. Fibro rooves would sometimes collapse giving off clouds of asbestos dust.

Graham asked me if I would offer evidence in support. Of course I answered in the affirmative. His lawyer sent me Graham's statement and asked me if I agreed with its contents. I replied that I thought it was conservative in its detail and if I had to make a statement it would probably be stronger than that. Graham knew that if his case was successful, he would not live long enough to enjoy any benefits, but he wanted the win for his family. Once again, the matter never went to court. The fire service paid the money. How could they possibly argue the case?

Chapter 8. Gender (In) equality.

During Geoff Skerritt's term as Fire Service Commissioner, a new TV show appeared with the support of the Q FS. It was called "Fire". The story revolved around the introduction of a female firefighter into an entirely male fire service. It was made with the support and assistance of Brisbane fire service resources, frequently resources we could not afford to lend. The script and the dialogue was ridiculous; every member of the fire service in the show had ridiculous nicknames and their behaviour was completely unacceptable and foreign to anybody who genuinely works in the service. I tried to watch it, I really did, but after about 10 minutes I had to turn it off; it just made me angry.

As duty officer at Roma Street, outstations would telephone me at the start of every shift to report in and confirm their shift strengths. I remember one station calling me and saying, "Dinosaur's here, and there's a bloke standing behind the fridge with his cock hanging out." This was the effect that this TV show had on everybody; it either made you angry or you laughed at it. The result of the plot was predictable; the new female recruit overcame every obstacle and became a shining success.

Coincidentally, and I'm sure it was just a coincidence, two new female applicants were about to try out for admission to the Q FS. On the day they were due to attempt to pass the tests, Commissioner Skerritt and Regional Commander Bartlett arrived at the training centre. This was a routine procedure of applicants trying out to be probationary recruits, yet for some reason it attracted the attendance of the Commissioner and a regional commander. One of the tests involved handling a charged line of hose. Fire service hoses are over 60 mm in diameter and carry a large amount of water under high pressure. Being able to handle a fire hose is about as basic a requirement for a firefighter as you can think of. The pump operator in this case was a fireman named Jack Tinsley. Jack was a man who could not be coerced or bullied and would not fake anything. As the female recruits were about to get their turn on the fire hose, Bartlett approached Jack and said, "Jack you can take a break if you like." Jack replied, "No thanks I'm fine." Jack had to be ordered off the pump and he went up to the messroom and watched from the veranda. When you carry out this exercise with all circumstances the same, i.e. the same length of hose, the same water pressure, et cetera, you can predict within a few centimetres where the water will fall after it leaves the hose in every case. Suddenly Jack noticed that when the female recruits were having their turn, the water seemed to fall much shorter. This can only mean that the pressure (what should be about 600kpa) must have been reduced. These female recruits were going to make it by any means necessary.

This sort of gender bias continued for some time; an officer I knew was training new recruits including one that was sent down from a country town. She weighed about 50 kg and took a size 3 boot. He discovered that he could not put her on the end of a charged line of hose because she would leave the ground. He knew he could not terminate her although if it was a male recruit the man would have been advised to seek another career. The probationary period was concluded and the female recruit was sent back to her hometown, leaving us to wonder how she ever passed the recruitment tests. That fire service then had a firefighter that could not use a fire hose. It's like having a carpenter who could not use a hammer.

One other TV show that appeared about same time was something called "Police Rescue". Rescue work is a large part of what firefighters do and it requires proper technique and training. I saw one episode where there was a large spill of drums of unidentified liquid where the member of the police rescue squad was standing on top of these drums, his blue overalls unbuttoned at the top to show off his manly chest, wondering what he should do next. If the contents were anything like some of the spills that we encountered, he wouldn't have to wonder, he would be dead. It was another show that I avoided because for somebody that is trained in proper procedure in any such emergencies, the script was ridiculous.

Female applicants for probation were not a new experience; several had tried on previous occasions when the testing procedure was carried out at Roma Street Station. They were given every assistance but they couldn't make it. During the making of this terrible TV show and what followed, it was obvious that the management were determined that this failure would be overcome. During the making of the TV show, a fire service pump was made available every day, whether we could afford it or not.

On 7 November 94, C shift ceased duty at 08:00 hours for a four-day break. This was in the middle of frequent fire activity such as we often see in our community. In the afternoon of the seventh, a fireman named Frank Bowman realised that his home was threatened by fire. He rang three times asking for fire service assistance but was told, sorry, we have nothing to send; pump 402 is making movies. All of C shift was off duty and available from the seventh for four days. Frank and his family managed to save his home but he lost stables and fences. Nothing was more important than the making of this terrible TV show.

Chapter 9. Mundingburra.

MUNDINGBURRA WAS THE KEY ELECTORATE THAT CHANGED THE GOVERNMENT IN 1996. It was the reason that I was approached by Leo Keliher, and it was the reason that many of the predators that were constantly pursuing me were removed from office.

The Brisbane branch of the UFU wanted to make some sort of a statement in this electorate that might have some impact on the election. They put together a committee of members, and the committee included me. We decided, with branch approval, to insert a full-page ad in the local newspaper. I arranged for the ad to appear in the Townsville Bulletin on the day of the election, and coincidentally it appeared on the page opposite an ad for the Labour Party candidate. The big print in the Brisbane branch UFU ad said, "Don't Get Burnt!". I paid the bill for the ad.

The Two-Pronged Attack (Parliament And Trade Union).

After the election, the details of the ad were presented to the Brisbane branch, a vote of thanks was passed, and I was reimbursed at the meeting by Kevin Brazel, the State union secretary. Two things happened in the weeks that followed: –

1. I was personally attacked in parliament by Robert Schwarten;
2. Henry Lawrence, assistant secretary in the UFU at the time, made a complaint against me to the CJC. Let's deal with these one at a time.

Robert Schwarten, a member of the legislative assembly, decided to make use of his position in parliament to attack me personally. He alleged that I was part of some sort of memorandum of understanding to do with the election, and that I had made some personal arrangements with a woman called Wendy Armstrong, who I believe was a bureaucrat, but I don't know in what position. I had the opportunity to reply, and I made these arrangements through the speaker of the house. It is known as "citizen's right of reply", and the first one ever to be presented to Parliament in Queensland was mine, citizens right of reply number one. In my right of reply I declared that none of his allegations were correct and I did not have any idea where he got his suppositions from. The right of reply was read out in parliament.

Undeterred, Mr Schwarten responded with another attack on me. I found the nearest Labour Party member of Parliament to me, Mr Dean Wells. I visited his office, put down a transcript of Mr. Schwarten's slander, and expressed my displeasure (that's as polite a description as I can make in print). Mr Wells assured me he would talk to Schwarten and make sure he stopped. I said, "that's not good enough. Book me in to see him." During the meeting I had with Mr Schwarten he accepted that none of the allegations he had made were correct and he assured me he would correct the matter in the house. I must've missed that particular piece of Hansard. For the record, I say now as I said then, I had no role in any memorandum of understanding if there was one, I did not know anybody called Wendy Armstrong, in fact the first time I ever heard the name was when it came from the mouth of Robert Schwarten. I have never met Wendy Armstrong, and that is still the case today.

A word to Mr Schwarten. The work that firefighters do can often be dangerous, uncomfortable, and exhausting. The work that firefighters do is often carried out under a great deal of stress leading to personal trauma and anxiety. It is very different to the world of state parliament and air-conditioned comfort and privilege. At the end of our respective terms of service, the superannuation of firefighters pales into insignificance when compared to the pay-off of a politician. Nevertheless, we seem to be rated much higher in the public eye than politicians. The public seem to afford us a great deal of respect. I believe, Mr Schwarten, that you should follow their example. The firefighters I speak of, Mr Schwarten, includes me.

Henry Lawrence made a complaint to the CJC about the ad we put in the Townsville bulletin, saying he did not know who authorised it and he was worried that it might have been paid for by union funds. As I have said in the script above, the ad was authorised by the Brisbane branch of the UFU, it was initially paid for by me, and I was reimbursed the money by Kevin Brazel, Henry's boss, at a Brisbane branch meeting, and it was all recorded in the branch minutes. This means one of three things: – Henry did not read branch minutes, Henry did not consult with Kevin Brazel, his boss, or he lied to the CJC.

I was visited at home by a plainclothes police officer named Sgt Reeves with a tape recorder hanging over his shoulder. He asked me questions about this matter, and I told him I could not help him with his investigation. An enquiry had been set up by the outgoing government chaired by Commissioner Carruthers, and I was subpoenaed to appear. As I recall, one other fireman, fireman Roger Williams, was also subpoenaed. I gave Roger some simple advice; take your time, tell the truth, and don't embellish.

Within the Carruthers enquiry, you looked down from the witness box at a squadron of silks in the front row. You had no knowledge of which of those might be there to make you look bad.

During my time in the witness box, Commissioner Carruthers looked at me and said, "who designed this ad and put it in the Townsville Bulletin?" I said, "I did." He said, "it's very good." I said, "thank you very much." Much laughter in the court.

During the questioning, it became apparent that my telephone had been monitored, that is to say they had a list of what calls I made and when. Particularly, they were interested in the fact that there was communication between me and my brother and between my brother and the Townsville bulletin. I replied that my brother and I are the only members of our family and from time to time we have to discuss family business. Also, because of his position as president of the police union, he is very busy and any phone calls he might make are not necessarily in any particular order, and any phone call might not have any relationship with the one taken previously. Every day I was there, I was watched closely by Leo Keliher, obviously hoping that I would say something that he could make use of. On the last day that I attended, as I left he was standing outside and I smiled at him and said, "see you later Leo." He replied, "yes Bruce, you certainly will." I assume Leo was not very happy with me or the progress in the Carruthers enquiry.

While this business was going on, I received an advice from the Queensland Police Credit Union, where I had an account, that my records had been seized by order of Pierre Mark Le-Grand, the head of the CJC. Whatever Pierre was looking for, he must have been very disappointed. There was nothing in the records of my account that were improper.

Chapter 10. The Vanishing File.

ABOUT THE TIME WHEN WE WERE RECEIVING A NEW STATE GOVERNMENT, a copy of George Malouf's timesheet came into my possession covering the period immediately after the appeals fiasco before Brian Walsh. Malouf and I were both stationed at Roma Street and Malouf had trouble coming to work; on-duty staff looked at him as if he was dogs vomit, so he took about three weeks off. He put in a claim for this time off as workers compensation, saying he had injured his back at an incident and could not walk. The trouble was, George wasn't smart enough to stay home. He lived at New Farm at the time and would travel to Kemp Place fire station, telephone Peter George who was his second in charge and who would dutifully travel to Kemp Place to receive his instructions for the day. George was seen walking around the yard at Kemp Place, bending down talking to people through their car windows, without any apparent distress.

Workers Compensation placed George Malouf under surveillance; I believe it was the first and only time a working senior fire officer was placed under surveillance. When they had seen enough, they called him into the office and told him they would not pay him, but if he wished he could go to a doctor of their choice. Malouf was not going to do that. He went to Alan Bartlett and told him of the problem. Malouf's timesheet was changed; the bad back became acute sinusitis and the workers compensation became sick pay. Workers compensation fraud is a serious offence and will usually lead to charges. George Malouf was not charged because they caught him before he got the money.

When I received evidence of this, I took it to Peter George who was now Area Director. He got a serious shock, and I said, "this is too big for you Peter, you better book me in to see Wayne Hartley." Wayne Hartley was by now the Commissioner.

When Hartley saw the timesheet, he said, "what do you want? Do you want money?" I said," the amount of money that I lost in this incident is small, I didn't do anything wrong, I want my personal file corrected to indicate that." He said, "leave it with me."

I received a letter from Wayne Hartley telling me that my personal file could not be found and he could do no more. I waited a few months, telephoned Fire Brigade headquarters at Kedron Park, and spoke to a station officer who was working there. He was an import from Melbourne, and did not know any of the history. I said to him, "I've got to come up there for another matter, while I'm there I might have a look at my personal file, would you pull it out for me?" He said, "yes certainly."

When I arrived, there it was, the phantom file, as thick as a telephone book. Inside the file, dutifully stamped "to be filed" was a copy of the letter sent to me by Wayne Hartley telling me he could not find my file. An officer close by was Trevor Carney. I told him I wanted a copy of it. He said, "what part？" I said, "all of it. If I take my eyes off it it will disappear again." So I stood there using one of their many copying machines and retrieving the evidence.

While I was standing there, I had to consider how far down the fire service had become from the days of the Brisbane Metropolitan Fire Brigade to the now government run Queensland Fire Service.

George Malouf, I believe, was rewarded With an Australian Fire Service Medal.

The appointment of Wayne Hartley as Commissioner is in itself an interesting episode. When applications were called for the position of Commissioner, there were only two realistic applicants worth considering. One of them was Keith Drummond, the last Chief Officer of the Brisbane Fire Brigade and currently serving as regional commander. The other candidate was Wayne Hartley, and he was a candidate because of recent positions he found himself in. The Minister decided to do a study and review of the fire service, putting this matter in the hands of a lady named Lynn Staib. To assist her in this endeavour, she was given the help of Wayne Hartley. Consequently, these two remained in close contact for some considerable time carrying out this responsibility. I believe, by the time the review was finished, Miss Staib believed that Wayne Hartley was probably the best officer in Queensland. There was of course a formal selection process, but everybody knows that appointments at this level are controlled by the cabinet of the government of the day. Anything that might have happened in the cabinet room is of course not known to me, so I must speculate on the possibilities.

Premier Rob Borbidge had a majority of one, very slender. The Minister for the fire service was Mick Veivers, a man of extensive parliamentary experience and one who knew all the tricks that might be employed. He would have been advised by Miss Staib that in her opinion Wayne Hartley was the best man for the job. He might have gone into the cabinet room and decided to use the numbers; that is this very slender majority, to get his own way. He might have said, "this is our man (Hartley) and if we don't have him I'll resign and you won't have a government." Did he do that? I don't know. I realise, knowing what I do know about politics, that it has to be considered as a possibility. I only know, as time demonstrated, that we did not get the best man for the job.

Chapter 11. The pre-scripted promotion saga.

IN 1997, because of a number of retirements leaving some senior vacancies, a program was put in place that would allow qualified officers to apply for senior positions. Everything was properly structured, application forms inviting qualifications of applicants, selection criteria to be addressed by each applicant, but in fact the people that the fire service management wanted in these positions had already been selected.

The most glaring example of this was an application by Colin Hartley. Hartley had told everybody that he would get any senior position he wanted because his brother was the Commissioner. That turned out to be the case. Selection criteria 3 asked of the applicant, "Demonstrated ability to implement fire service operations management control and large-scale urban and rural fires and other emergency incidents." In his reply to SC3, he wrote, "I have been directly involved in many large fires and incidents as either the fire commander or regional mobilising officer together with some of the largest loss of life in the history of the Q FS, namely the Whiskey Au-Go-Go nightclub fire." I found this an extraordinary claim considering that the fire had occurred in 1973 and, Colin Hartley joined the fire service as a junior fireman in 1971.

Investigation told me that the senior officer in charge of this fire was a man named Ted Kropp and the first station officer to attend was Keith Drummond, who would later become Chief Officer of the Brisbane Fire Brigade. Keith Drummond told me that Hartley did indeed attend the fire as a junior fireman, it was the first time he had ever seen a fatality, (15 people died in that fire) and he threw up into the face piece of his breathing apparatus, and had to be told to sit on the curb with his head down. I launched an appeal which was heard by a panel including those people who were responsible for the promotions and Colin Hartley himself. I exposed this lie in his application, he looked at the table and said, "Bruce Wilkinson's made some allegations about me, and I refute them, and that's all I have to say." In other words, he had nothing to say that would explain his false claim.

In the same selection criteria, Hartley also claims credit for the management of a particularly large fire that occurred some years later. His submissions states, "I was directly involved with the very large Salisbury cotton and tyre fire as the regional mobilising officer and had arrived on site the second day when the fire had rapidly spread. I was one of only three senior officers with communication and mobilised additional pump units to bring the fire spread back under control with some 27 units." This fire became known in the fire service as the fine cotton fire, associating it with a notorious horserace and a disastrous result.

Colin Hartley was not in charge of this fire, during his attendance he was second in charge to George Malouf. Hartley and Malouf had arrived in the morning when the fire had been brought under control through the night by the management of Chief Officer Keith Drummond. When Malouf was given control of the incident, the fire was restricted to a large tyre dump with a warehouse of cotton neighbouring the fire. In the hours that followed, Malouf and Hartley lost control of the fire with the result that the entire warehouse of cotton was lost. Hartley was screaming into the radio that they had a firestorm. What they had was a fire out of control because they neglected to check the weather report for the day. It took several days to regain control of the fire with the renewed management of the chief officer.

During this appeals hearing, if you were winning arguments with the people in the panel, they would ask you to wait outside while they considered what they probably needed to say, and then invite you back inside.

The appeal, the exposure of the false claim, made no difference. I don't think anything would have made any difference. Before the applications were made, I had an interview with a senior officer called Reg Christensen. He told me that your written application would be forwarded to your senior officer for study, so, as he said, "if you lie, we'll know about it." Hartley's application went to his senior officer, Peter George. Peter's written response began, "I joined the job with Col----". This means that Peter George must've known as I did that Colin Hartley could not possibly have been in charge at the Whiskey-a-go-go fire. Even when the lie was exposed, it didn't make any difference. All people who had been preselected for the positions were promoted, regardless of the quality or the accuracy of their applications or any appeals.

Colin Hartley became another of my dedicated pursuers. Any and every decision I made that might be challenged was carefully studied by a number of people including Colin Hartley. On one occasion, when I was acting as a Senior Operations Coordinator, there was a motor vehicle accident south of Brisbane. Hartley immediately wrote a report demanding to know why I had not attended that accident. I studied the map and replied that the motor vehicle accident was in the Gold Coast region and he might wish to direct his query to the SOC on the Gold Coast. I heard no more.

Eventually I received a formal response from the chairman of the appeals Tribunal. The front page of such a response establishes the integrity of the response and the appeals process. The front page of the response that I received was terribly inaccurate. It quoted people in attendance that were not there. The formal response that I received was in fact on a par with the whole process.

Chapter 12. The Underground Newspaper.

DURING THE REIGN OF LEO KELIHER as Director-General of emergency services, a newspaper emerged called "CODE=INE". Its purpose was to expose every mistake, every negligent decision that was expensive to the fire service, every secret deal made between the management of the union and the director-general, and anything else that the rank and file should know about.

It was well written, clever, and highly sought after. Every fireman wanted to read CODE=INE before anything else, including the Courier Mail. It did serious damage to the credibility of the union leadership at that time and the senior leadership of the fire service. It was also anonymous. Some senior executives in the union tried to confiscate any copies that appeared in the fire station without success. There were attempts by the union executive and the government to find the authors, without success.

A complaint was made to the police and a routine investigation was carried out. I was a suspect, and I was interviewed by a police officer about the matter. George Malouf said, "I knew it wasn't you, I've read your reports and you don't write that good." I said to myself, "for once, thank you George for your great intelligence and perception." I can say now, as I said then, I had no part in the production of this journal. Anything I ever wrote had my name on the bottom.

The continual editions of this newspaper caused great damage to those people in power who were trying to maintain a respectable image and control of the fire service at the same time. Coincidentally, some senior positions were about to be available through the usual application process. If you were interested you had to apply for the proper application forms from Forbes house, the fire service headquarters at that time.

I do not know who the authors of CODE=INE were, and neither does anybody else with certainty, but there were many educated guesses and suppositions. The two people who I believe may have been responsible for the production of this outstanding piece of journalism shall now be referred to in this chapter by aliases, because I have no proof that they were indeed the writers. We'll call them the professor and the ego.

I got a phone call from a member of our staff telling me that the professor and the ego had been seen at a coffee shop very close to Forbes house, formally attired and looking as though they were ready for an interview. I called the professor and asked him what he was doing there on that day. He told me he and the ego had gone into Forbes house to collect the application papers relevant to senior appointment. I pointed out to him that he could download these papers on the net, exactly like everybody else did including me. He replied, "Oh no I don't trust that. I've got to be sure that I will get the papers, so I went in to collect them personally." The professor was a very intelligent man and computer literate, much better with this sort of equipment than me or most of the other operational staff, but this was his alibi for being there.

Two things happened after their visit to Forbes house. Both the professor and the ego were promoted to senior rank, and the production of CODE=INE ceased. It is a remarkable coincidence and leads me to speculate that there may have been a deal done on that day between these two men and senior bureaucrats in the fire service. CODE=INE was never seen again.

Chapter 13. The Counterfeit Commissioner.

TOWARDS THE VERY END OF 2014, in fact on December 20, a newspaper article appeared In the Courier Mail. The article reported on an investigation and report written by a bureaucrat named Margaret Allison. The report alleged widespread misogynist and sexist culture throughout the Queensland Fire Service. The reason given for the report was a matter that happened in the Gold Coast fire service. There had been, I am told, a relationship in the Gold Coast fire service between two firefighters, one male and one female (you have to make that stipulation these days). The relationship terminated, and I believe the parting was acrimonious, as such partings often are. What happened between and by the two parties I don't know, but whatever they did seems to be the basis of the rumours, investigation, and report.

Ms Allison widened her net to include all of the Queensland Fire Service. Senior officers in Brisbane went out to interview all female firefighters they had in their area, as they should. They asked these firefighters two questions: –

1. Have you ever experienced improper behaviour from any staff either verbally or physically?
2. Has anybody interviewed you on this subject?

In every case, the answer to both questions was no.

Brisbane, because of its size, has more female fire staff than any other area. The answers to the questions put to the staff by senior officers puts considerable doubt on the accuracy of Ms Allison's report. The article in the Courier Mail, which faithfully reported the key points of Ms Allison's report, was written at the perfect time for anything that might be questioned or challenged; exactly 5 days before Christmas. It was written by Steven Wardill, a man who I'm sure would describe himself as an investigative journalist, the key word here being investigative.

The report and its public exposure through the Courier Mail placed Fire Service Commissioner Lee Johnson in an impossible position. Regarding the matter on the Gold Coast, he had asked senior officers in charge in that area about the matter, and he had been advised that everything was in hand. Nevertheless, this report and its public revealing left Lee Johnson believing that he had to resign his position.

The report had one other result in the fire service. It created a great deal of distrust.

Many of us connected to the fire service have asked why did Ms Allison write the report, who commissioned her to write it, and for what purpose? Any time a report is written or commissioned by a politician or bureaucrat it is intended that the report will say exactly what they wanted when it was commissioned.

I have not read Ms Allison's report; I do not read much fiction. I relied on the article in the Courier mail written by Steven Wardill, trusting that his report in the paper would be an accurate reflection of Ms Allison's work.

Some have speculated about the reason for this report. Premier Campbell Newman was not doing well in the polls and a state election was not too far away. Shortly after Lee Johnson resigned his post, Katarina Caroll, a police woman, was appointed as an Acting Commissioner. Did Premier Newman believe that this extreme example of political correctness would boost his ratings? If so, it backfired badly. Every firefighter, their families and their extended social groups were offended and alienated by this plot. I spoke to senior officers that I knew and used to work with, and I said to them, "what will you do if you get something big? She won't know what she's doing." They replied, "yes we know that, but we won't let that happen." This means, in the event of a large emergency, she would be insulated from the action and the decision-making, and she would mostly appear on the television, on formal occasions, and in the Courier mail.

Mr Wardill, I ask you, don't immediately print anything that is given to you by politicians or bureaucrats. Investigate the matter and verify every sentence. Frequently what you might receive from such people could politely be described as bovine faeces.

I wrote to Mrs Caroll when she was first appointed, and told her that she was not qualified for the job and shouldn't be there. She replied that it was all legal. I found that a strange remark, and I'm not sure that indeed it was all legal.

After the election and we had a new government, my local member of Parliament was Shane King. I took this matter up to his office, put the details on his desk and said, "What do you think of that?" He replied, "It's terrible." I asked, "What are you going to do about it?" He replied, "I'll pass it on to the Minister." I believed, because it was Campbell Newman's decision and this was a government on the other side of the political spectrum, that they would change it. I underestimated the feminist push of our new Premier.

I received a letter from the Minister, Jo-anne Miller, telling me that she would search all of Australia for the best possible candidate for the Commissioner's office. When I received the letter, she had already permanently appointed Mrs Caroll as Fire Service Commissioner. It was the fastest search of Australia in the history of our country.

A new Commissioner has been appointed, Mr Greg Leach. Mr Leach has had 33 years experience in this profession, and is widely accepted as being well-qualified for the position. I guess when Jo-Anne Miller was making her wide search of Australia for the best possible candidate, Mr Leach must've been overlooked. Or possibly, Jo-Anne Miller might have considered Katarina Caroll better qualified for the job.

The probability is, when you look at the Fire Service Act, her permanent promotion was illegal. The fire service act under the section Commissioner, clause 2, says: –

A person who does not have professional experience in fire prevention and firefighting is not eligible for appointment as Commissioner.

If you look at the act now that clause has been removed. Perhaps the government is trying to hide its previous indiscretions, but the clause was there when Mrs Caroll was appointed.

The removal of this clause raises other serious concerns; it means that the government of the day can appoint anybody in their favour to the position of Fire Service Commissioner, a retired officer from the defence Force, someone who has giving good service to the party, a member of Parliament, or a prominent bureaucrat. Any of these choices would mean that the Commissioner would have to be separate from operational activity.

Not too long after this appointment, a vacancy became available for Commissioner of Police. I knew of course that Commissioner Caroll would apply. I tried to place a bet on her success in winning this position, but I could not find anybody that would take the bet.

What we have seen are two consecutive, history making, successful senior appointments. Does anybody believe that gender was the principal qualification in awarding these two appointments?

Me too.

Chapter 14. Fire service legislation (the vandalism of)

SEVERAL CHANGES HAVE BEEN MADE TO THE FIRE SERVICE ACT since the fire service come under control of the government and its bureaucrats. We have already looked at the removal of the key clause that qualifies applications for the appointment of the commissioner. Other clauses deal with the responsibility of the police, or rather the establishment that now under the Fire Service Act they have no responsibility.

In part IX----general

136 (1) and (2) used to say: — it is the duty of the police to assist the Commissioner.

1. upon receiving information of the occurrence of a fire or chemical incident requiring the attendance of officers of the Queensland Fire Service, theCommissioner of Police or the member of the police force in charge, at the time, of the police station nearest to the location of the fire or chemical incident must immediately send members of the police force in sufficient number to preserve order and to assist at the fire or chemical incident.
2. it is the duty of every member of the police force present at a fire or chemical incident to assist any officer of the Queensland Fire service who is discharging functions and exercising powers under this act.

152. Power of police to arrest without warrant. Where a member of the police force believes on reasonable grounds that a person –

(A) has failed to comply with a requisition made pursuant to paragraph (J) or (K) of section 53 (2);
or
(B) (B) has failed to comply with a requisition made pursuant to section 57 (1) in respect of name or address;
or
(C) (C) has committed an offence defined in section 92 or 147 (1) (a); the member may arrest the person without warrant and take the person before a justice to be dealt with according to law.

These clauses have disappeared. There is no longer any reference in the fire service act to the police force and their responsibility to assist. I know from my experience in working with the police on many occasions, that any police officer I have worked with would not need to be obliged under the law to assist in such emergencies. Nevertheless, it is logical for such requirements to be spelt out in the law, to be included in instructions to all emergency services including the police so that there is not even a lingering doubt with a new recruit about what he should or should not do.

All my experience in 35 years at emergencies, public appearances and conferences with the police have been agreeable, harmonious, and the display of an obvious willingness to help. In any such close agreeable relationship, occasionally you can have a slight disagreement. I relate here one such isolated episode.

While serving as a duty officer at Roma Street, at the start of the shift, I found myself one man short. Normally, anybody who is not going to arrive will phone in sick or whatever, where the duty officer will hold back a man from the off going shift until he is able to fill the vacancy. In this case, I had no advice and I found myself one man short in the crews. I waited, telling my on shift staff to man whatever appliance might be called out until I solved the problem. After about 15 minutes I received a phone call from my missing man, and I barked into the phone, "where the hell are you?" He replied, "I'm in the watch house." "What happened?" He told me he had been to a bucks party the night before, had stayed the night believing it was the right thing for him to do, and in the morning, travelling to work, he was stopped by a breathalyser squad. Not only did he still apparently read over, but according to them, he did not have a drivers license. The man's name was Jones, which probably gives an indication of why they made this mistake. I should make note the man was in fire service uniform, and he would have told them that he was on his way to work at Roma Street, a short walk from the watch house.

Nevertheless, he was incarcerated. I asked was there a police officer there, and he gave the phone to the attending officer. I said, "who am I talking to?" And the answer came, "Constable Newman Sir." I said, "I'm the duty officer at Roma Street fire station and you've got one of my men which means I'm a man short and an emergency vehicle is unavailable. Return my man to Roma Street Station immediately." He replied, "I can't do that sir I've only got a motorbike."

I Called the crew of first pump, gave them a walkie-talkie (the other one was going to be on my duty office desk) told them to drive to the watch house, park the pump across the gate, and don't come back until you've got Jones. I also told them that all communication was to be via walkie-talkie and not through the radio.

They did return with Jones; apparently a sergeant had returned and immediately knew what should be done. I then had another problem. If I believed that fireman Jones was under the influence, I could not allow him to be on duty. I summoned a transport utility and driver and sent fireman Jones up to the Royal Brisbane Hospital to be tested. They determined indeed that fireman Jones was not under the influence of alcohol and could therefore start work. I asked him if he wished to contest the DUI charge, and I would be prepared to give evidence on his behalf. He declined, saying no I'll just pay the money and forget about it.

Chapter 15. Smoke Alarm Fiasco.

IN 2016, new smoke alarm legislation was passed through the house of Parliament. This was brought about by a terrible disaster that happened in 2011 In Slacks Creek. This house fire resulted in the death of 11 people. There were two reasons for this terrible loss of life: –

1. The house was overcrowded; too many people in one ordinary domestic dwelling.
2. There was no operating fire alarm at all in this house. One operating smoke alarm would have alerted the residents for an early evacuation.

As a result of this terrible loss of life, a committee was formed of local people. These were civic minded, conscientious people who wanted to make a change, but none of them had any knowledge at all of fire alarms or anything to do with the fire service. What they have produced, with the best of intentions, is something that has to be changed.

When the legislation was first introduced and I became aware of it, I was doing voluntary work for the fire service, addressing groups on behalf of the fire service as they received requests for somebody to talk to them about fire safety. I wrote a list of questions regarding the new smoke alarm legislation, but did not get a reply.

Eventually, I had a meeting with a number of senior fire officers; inspectors, superintendents, and one assistant Commissioner. I asked them why they had not answered my questions, their reply was, "we've got hundreds of questions, we haven't got any answers."

We went through some of the questions I had put to them without any satisfactory result.

I asked, "how are you going to police this?" They replied, "we cannot." I said to them, "you understand that people are very concerned about this whole business, the cost, the legalities, and you understand when I answer their questions I'm not going to lie to them; I'm going to tell them the truth." They made no comment. I continued to conduct addresses to groups until I decided to discontinue my services.

While I was addressing groups on behalf of the fire service, I was frequently asked about the smoke alarm legislation; people were worried about the cost and the legalities and how it would affect them. I told them that some of the legislation had serious flaws and they should delay spending their money and making any changes because I believed one government or another would make changes to this legislation for the benefit of all Queenslanders. People came up to me after the session and told me how relieved they were to receive this advice.

The problems I have with this legislation are as follows: – the legislation demands that there is a smoke alarm in every bedroom and at each end of every hallway, and other positions considered necessary. This adds up to a lot of smoke alarms, and they are not the smoke alarms we are all used to in hardware stores. These smoke alarms have to be hardwired; that is to say, they all have to be connected to the AC power supply in the house and they will have to be interconnected, which means that if one goes off they will all go off. Many houses in Brisbane and other cities in Queensland have very a low pitched roof or a fibro roof containing asbestos which means that nobody can work in the ceiling space. This difficulty can be overcome by the use of Wi-Fi or by using special batteries in each individual alarm. All the smoke alarms have to have a battery fitted as a backup source of power. If these smoke alarms are interconnected by using Wi-Fi, considering the number of alarms that may be installed in a house, it may be necessary to install an alarm board such as you see in commercial premises. Whatever you need to install, it will need to be done by an electrician, unlike the standard smoke alarm that we are all used to that you can install yourself. All this means considerable expense inflicted on people who in many cases cannot afford it.

If elderly people pass away or have to vacate their house, will their family have to spend this money on what was the family home? If somebody does have a house fire and it is determined that smoke alarms were not installed, were not properly maintained, or were defective, will they be prosecuted?

If there is a fire, and it is determined that smoke alarms were not fitted and maintained exactly according to legislation, will this be used by insurance companies to avoid payment?

What are the advantages to the community from this legislation? None.

All of the smoke alarms have to have a battery even though the legislation demands that they be hardwired. Obviously, when we encounter power failure over a large area, as we often do in storm season, the battery in the smoke alarm is what we depend on. There is no advantage to the operation of a smoke alarm because of the power source; any smoke alarm will operate efficiently whether the power is coming from a battery or from house wiring. At a time when we have blackouts from heavy storm activity, the possibility of a failure in the AC supply which might lead to a fire means we depend on the battery supply at a time when a problem is most likely.

Any smoke alarm that you can buy at a hardware store for not much money and install yourself will contain a battery that will last for at least a year. We used to advise people to pick a day in the year to change their battery; 1 April was a common choice, but any day will do, such as somebody's birthday, New Year's Day, as long as it is the same day every year. Every smoke alarm has a testing button prominently displayed, so that you can push this button with a broomstick and make sure it is working properly. If the battery is running low, the alarm will issue some slight noises to tell you that you should change the battery.

I have been to thousands of alarms in commercial premises involving smoke alarms. Smoke alarms, like all technology, can be faulty, and if you find a smoke alarm that needs to be replaced, in commercial premises you can isolate it on the control panel. If you have a smoke alarm that is faulty in the house in the middle of the night and you can't turn it off all of the smoke alarms will continue to operate until you can persuade some electrician to come and fix the problem for you.

For me personally, I will not be installing hardwired smoke alarms in my house. They would give me no advantage, they would cost me a substantial amount of money, and they may in fact give me some disadvantage. An ordinary smoke alarm, when operated, will be heard not only by everybody in your house but probably by people in the house next door. If one or two standard smoke alarms had been installed in that house at Slacks Creek and had been operational, that terrible tragedy in 2011 would probably have been avoided. There must be somebody in government who is prepared to consult with qualified people (experienced firefighters) and amend this legislation to save all Queenslanders a lot of unnecessary expense and put their minds at ease.

Chapter 16. Grand Larceny.

THIS IS PERHAPS THE BIGGEST INTENTIONAL THEFT BY AGENTS of a government in the history of Australia. It begins with the introduction of a 38 hour week for fire staff decreed in 1996 by the Queensland Industrial Relations Commission. The problem immediately facing the management of the fire service and the Queensland government was the implementation of this decree.

The fire service operates 24 hours a day, it is an essential service and cannot, like commercial enterprises, simply close its doors after 38 hours has passed for the week. The operating on-shift fire staff at that time were working a 10/14 roster, which meant that they worked an average of 42 hours a week. Changing the roster, shortening working hours to deliver 38 hours a week, would mean hiring more staff and increasing considerably the remuneration budget. After some negotiation and discussion, the following package was determined: – two hours per week would be repaid by adjustment to annual leave; the other two hours would be paid as a two hours per week payment which became slyly referred to by the management as "the 38 hour week allowance". The management decided, in collaboration with agents of the government, to exclude this payment from superannuation entitlements. There was much debate about this matter and many lies were told;" the unions agreed to exclude it from superannuation" (not true)." The cost to the fire service would add a great load on the annual fire service budget "(this means that whether or not you should pay something depends entirely on whether you can afford it). There were letters of protest from all of the relevant Unions to no avail.

When I was looking at retirement, I attended the office of Q-Super to gain a retirement figure. I also took up a payslip which clearly showed the separate amount paid for these two hours per week. They were able to tell me the amount of money that this two hours, included in my superannuation calculations, would be worth. The approximate figure on my retirement for these two hours was $20,000. When I did retire, the aforementioned figure was not included. All protests and correspondence about this matter gained me nothing. I drafted a petition protesting about this matter and demanding payment of the money that I was owed. This petition gained many signatures from serving firefighters and it was served on the chair of the Q-Super board of trustees, one Gerard Bradley, who I believe was working in Treasury for Premier Anna Bligh in his main job. I suppose the petition was unexpected, because we did not receive a reply for seven months. The reply, when it did arrive, made use of the original definition of the two hours describing it as "an allowance" and depending on the inadequate wording of the trust deed. By this time I had already sent a written detailed complaint to the Superannuation Complaints Tribunal in Melbourne.

The consideration and deliberation by the Tribunal took 2 1/2 years; bureaucrats do not work quickly. When the reply did come, they clearly defined what should be considered superannuable, that is to say, all of the hours that are worked on a regular basis, which means that I should have received superannuation for these two hours. The letter then states, "from the information we have received, these two hours are not worked and therefore cannot be included in superannuation calculations". This was a lie intentionally fed to the Tribunal to avoid Q-Super's and the government's commitments. Unfortunately, the Tribunal did not give me the opportunity to review this material before they made their decision; it would have been easy for me to demonstrate the falseness of this statement.

After consultation with a colleague of mine who had the same rank and similar length of service, we resubmitted another application to Superannuation Complaints Tribunal under the name of my colleague, Brian Donnelly. Another 2 1/2 years passed, and we received another decision; this time the decision was divided. Apparently, two members of the tribunal adjudicated on Brian Donnelly's submission. One of them was a member of the previous decision on my case, and apparently she was unwilling to admit that she got it wrong. The other member, Mr Ross Christie, immediately saw the truth of the matter and wrote very strongly that we should be paid, including whatever interest should be calculated for the time lost. I will quote Mr Christie: – "what is clear from the letter dated 9 August 2007 from the human resource director of the employer is that the statement made that the "38 hour week allowance" is not payment for hours worked is wrong." Mr Christie goes on to say, "This information which was finally provided by the Trustee is consistent with the original submission made by the complainant. It is disappointing that the Trustee in its submission quoted the section of the previous determination that the 38 hour week allowance was not a payment for hours worked with its implied agreement when it knew or should have known that such statement was incorrect." This is about as strong a statement as somebody in Mr Christie's position could make without actually saying that the human resource director, whoever he was (and I would like to know who he was) was actually lying to save the government money.

So what happens next? We have two members of the Tribunal with completely opposite results. I was told by somebody who worked in the Tribunal that on such an occasion one of the two people would be appointed as chair of the meeting, and that chair would have a casting vote. If our application had been heard on a different day when Mr Christie was in the chair, we would have received a favourable result.

An investigation of the Superannuation Resolution of Complaints Act 1993 reveals the following: –

> 25. Power to obtain information and documents. Subsection (6) must not fail to comply with the requirement made by the Tribunal under subsections (1), (2) or (3) (provision of information). This section carries strict liability with reference to the criminal code. It is possible that in knowingly giving false information to the Tribunal, the human resource director may have committed a criminal offence. Further: –

(5) if the members constituting the Tribunal disagree on a determination to be made by the Tribunal, a decision of the majority is taken to be a decision of all of them.

To fulfil the definition of "majority" it appears for the sake of convenience that one member of the Tribunal had two votes and the other had one. For most people, this could hardly be defined as a majority.

Any correspondence to the Tribunal after the decision is made brings a reply saying that the Tribunal cannot revisit a matter that has already been determined.

The CEO of Q-Super at that time was Rosemary Vilgan. I wrote to Ms Vilgan on a number of occasions spelling out the obvious truth and asking her to correct this injustice. Put simply, she didn't want to know about it. The replies that I got simply reiterated the previous false statements that had been made by other people representing the government. In the last letter that I received from Ms Vilgan, she told me that if I wrote again she would not reply. She was not going to engage in any sort of discussion where she would be proven to be wrong.

Everyone knows the Q-super add with lady looking out the window at the rain. If that lady was a retired firefighter, she would not be smiling. She would be crying. In 2008, I actually achieved a brief television interview exposing this theft and appealing to the Parliament for my money. Shortly after, I had an interview with Commissioner Don Brown, Queensland Workplace Rights Ombudsman. After reviewing the matter, Commissioner Brown wrote to the Superannuation Complaints Tribunal on my behalf urging them to take another look at the applications of mine and Mr Donnelly's. I quote Commissioner Brown: – "In both determinations it would appear to me, on the information available, there may have been a misunderstanding of the so-called 38 hour week allowance. It is not an allowance paid for two hours time off, it is in fact the payment made for the 39th and 40th hours of work performed by Q FRS officers each and every week of work and in fact is also paid when offices are on leave." Further in his correspondence he says, "it would seem a preferable course of action to review these existing matters rather than require other fresh complainants." Commissioner

Brown's response was the same from theTribunal as the one that I had received; i.e. we cannot revisit a matter that has been dealt with.

Also in 2008, this disgraceful rip-off was exposed in the Queensland Parliament. By invitation, I attended Parliament and sat in the front row of the public gallery. MLA member Mark McArdle addressed the matter inviting Premier Anna Bligh to discuss the matter with me and correct this theft. She of course declined, saying that I could discuss the matter with one of her ministers. I never did get to meet one of her ministers, instead being fobbed off to a couple of bureaucrats for one or two meetings. Mark McArdle put out a press release on 24 April 2008 with the heading: – "Bligh avoids meeting retired firemen on super rip-off but secures King's Ransom for electoral rorter." It drew no attention from any of the representatives of the media; apparently it was not important enough.

I made an appeal to the Administrative Appeals Tribunal in 2018, spelling out the details of the entire matter, the money that we had been cheated out of, the lies that had been told to the Superannuation Complaints Tribunal and the refusal of Q-Super or the government to do anything about it. I pointed out that the Superannuation Complaints Tribunal was a federal body and would therefore fall under the umbrella of a review by their organisation. They did not want to deal with this matter. They replied asking me to quote the particular federal law that might give them the authority to deal with it. Finally I received a phone call from their Chief Oficer asking me to withdraw my application. Perhaps if I had been an illegal immigrant trying to avoid deportation I might have received a more favourable response.

Some attention should be paid to this matter by the federal government. I do not know in which portfolio the Superannuation Complaints Tribunal would fall, but it must be obvious they need to review their procedures. If they have been lied to which results in the wrong decision costing, in this case, retiring firefighters who have given their all for a lifetime protecting Australian citizens and saving thousands of dollars, surely once that lie and resultant injustice is exposed, the Tribunal must be able to go back to that case and correct their mistake.

Now, finally, the lie has been exposed by the government itself. There is a Queensland Fire and Emergency Service certified agreement 2016, available for anybody to see on the web. In this agreement part 4 – firefighters and station officers, the agreement states: –

29. Hours of work and rosters

> (A) the 10/14 roster will remain in place as the recognised shift roster for continuous shift workers.
> (B) the roster is worked over an eight week period based on two shifts of 10 hours on dayshift and two shifts of 14 hours on night shift.
> (C) this roster necesitates the working of an average 42 hours per week. Two hours of the average of 42 hours is credited towards additional leave for the firefighter or station officer to be taken at a time convenient for the employer.

Further in the agreement, it states: – 44. 38 hour week allowance

> (A) the 38 hour week was introduced by way of the payment of an allowance known as the 38 hour week allowance. 38 hour week allowance is paid in lieu of reducing ordinary working hours from 40 to 38 under the award.

The two hours work per week, referred to as the "38 hour week allowance", is now included in superannuation calculations.

I sent this information to the Superannuation Complaints Tribunal. I received the same response as before. After they have made a decision, they cannot revisit the matter. Even when the truth is self-evident, revealed in black-and-white in an agreement between the union and the government, even when there is no longer any doubt about the validity of my original claim, The Superannuation Complaints Tribunal refuses to correct their obvious terrible mistake, a mistake that cost many retiring firefighters thousands of dollars.

How is this possible? How can a bureaucrat on behalf of the government skim approximately $20,000 from the superannuation entitlements of retiring firefighters and be so completely confident that they will get away with it? Maybe it's because we really don't have a Westminster system of government in Queensland. The upper house was done away with by means of a criminal conspiracy approximately 100 years ago. Queensland has the only government in Australia without a house of review. You cannot appeal to any senators in Queensland, you cannot seek justice or the correction of such a terrible piece of larceny, such as happened here, with somebody who, in any other state, would be available for consultation in an upper house of parliament. So far, all I have left is to stay alive in the hope that one government or another will return my stolen money.

I believe that superannuation funds should be completely independent of any political influence. This is the nest egg belonging to people at the end of their working life so that they will have some security now that they have retired. This nest egg should not be available for the manipulation and plundering of bureaucrats or politicians.

CEOs of superannuation funds and people appointed to superannuation boards should not be appointed by the government of the day. People in such positions should be conspicuously independent of all government offices and immune from political influence.

I make an appeal here to our Premier, Anastacia Palaszczuk. Madam Premier, I ask you, having exhausted every other avenue in an attempt to retrieve my stolen money, can you use your authority to see that I am paid while I'm still alive?

Chapter 17. Interesting Jobs.

THE EMERGENCIES THAT I ATTENDED DURING MY 35 YEARS in the fire service include every possible emergency that can be thought of, but I have listed here some jobs which are totally different to each other and may demonstrate the considerable variety that officers in the fire service my have to deal with.

On Wednesday, 6 March 1996 I received a call at 0819 hrs while on duty at Roma Street to Mineral House, 41 George Street. Mineral House was like many other high-rise commercial buildings in the city. I responded with two pumps, and on arrival I was greeted by security staff who advised me of smoke on levels three and four. Investigation revealed heavy smoke on level 3 and confirmed that levels three and four had been evacuated. I immediately ordered complete evacuation of the building, which took some time because of the need for assistance for one man on crutches from the 15th floor. I set up a fresh air base on level 2 and we commenced fire action with extinguishers and breathing apparatus, at the same time ordering the attendance of two more pumps. The fire itself was extinguished at 0854 hrs, but the smoke in the building created another problem. Electrical systems in the building and the backup generators were all sufficiently damaged to prevent the use of any air-conditioning and venting systems. Ventilation had to be done manually, and windows in buildings like this are not normally meant to be opened and have to be opened by the use of allen keys. Unfortunately the size of the keys necessary for this operation varied from floor to floor.

The building was unusable for several days because of the electrical repair work that was required to make the building serviceable. The fire itself was not very large, but because of the environment in which it occurred, on the third level of a high-rise building in the city, it required extra attention. Approximately 1200 people were evacuated from this building; this is the nature of high-rise buildings. A Building on one block of dirt can contain the equivalent of the population of a town. This is simply an illustration of the type of difficulties that might be encountered in any fire in a high-rise building in the city. The best part about this incident is that there were no casualties and Fire Brigade attendance was limited to about three hours.

Now for something completely different.

While stationed at Taigum fire station we responded to a call on an acreage property in the back blocks of Carseldine. On arrival, towards the front of the block, a disused septic tank was obviously the area that required attendance. The lid of the tank had broken and a horse had fallen in. The owner of the property, demonstrating his affection for the horse, had jumped into the tank to keep the horse's head above, er, water. This septic tank, though no longer in use, still contained a large quantity of the material it was originally designed for.

We managed to put a strap behind the front legs of the horse, hooked it to the pump, and slowly but steadily extracted the valiant steed from his odorous predicament. I am usually a hands-on type of officer, but I must confess that in this case I was content to stand back a few paces and simply give instructions.

I am full of admiration for the owner of the horse. In jumping into the tank he showed complete disregard for his own welfare and personal aromatic sociability.

I attended a fire in the late 80s in the western suburbs of Brisbane; it was late evening, it was a fire inside the house, and it did minimal structural damage. The circumstances of the fire, the house and the occupant make it totally outside of the ordinary. The owner of the house was an elderly woman who lived on her own. Because of the frequent occurrence of home invasions in modern times, she had obviously felt insecure and had made sure that the house was locked up tight.

This created circumstances that were fatal and, ultimately, disfiguring. The lady was asleep in bed when the fire began, and under these circumstances, a totally locked-up house, the fire never progressed beyond its insipid stage. What it produced was considerable quantities of carbon monoxide gas which resulted in the death of the lady in bed. It also produced a continuing buildup of heat within the building, producing circumstances to the woman's body resembling cooking in an oven.

All wrinkles that mature people accumulate in their life were gone; the body of the lady was bloated and unlike anything that friends and family would be accustomed to. I was advised that her son was coming to the house. I knew I could not allow him to see his mother like that. I placed a fireman on guard at the gate with instructions not to let the man in the house when he arrived; he could simply tell him that the building was not safe. I suppose we could put this tragedy down to personal insecurity in the face of ever-increasing home invasions.

In late December 1989, shortly after midnight, I responded to a potential suicide at the top of the Story Bridge. I responded with a turntable ladder to be met with police officers and our fire service senior officer, acting superintendent Ross Bell. The young man at the top of the Story Bridge was as close to leaving the bridge and heading towards the concrete below as it is possible to get. At the very peak of the story Bridge, attached to the bridge, is a steal piece of pipe connected to a floodlight. When I arrived, the man was straddling the steel pipe. The police had blocked off the bridge both ends, and we extended the ladder to its maximum length within the the superstructure of the bridge. This enabled us to climb off the ladder onto the structure of the bridge close to our rescue target.

I asked police for information about the man; how old was he, what did they know about him, what were his interests, et cetera. They told me he was in his early 20s, his brother had been shot by police in Sydney in an incident some weeks before, and apparently he was a reasonable boxer. One of my crew, Brad Bryant, said to me, "I'll go up with you so that I can operate the ladder from the top." This was Brad's way of volunteering to go aloft with me without actually volunteering. It was typical of the men I had on my shift, I was very lucky to have the support of men like Bryant. We went aloft, Brad Bryant and I, gaining as much altitude as the turntable would give us, and climbed onto the superstructure of the bridge. What followed became a game of cat and mouse between the young man and us.

Conversation like, don't come any closer or I'll jump, just take it easy mate we want to help, what can we do for you, is there anything you want, et cetera. We were able to provide him with a pack of cigarettes and matches, followed by a short retreat. In the middle of this back and forth, Brad Bryant said to me, "I hope he comes down soon." I said, "why?" He replied, "I'm scared of heights." Typical fire service humour in the middle of a tense incident. Finally, after much discussion, he wanted to talk to a friend of his who lived on the south side of Brisbane. A police car was dispatched to ferry his mate. When the friend arrived, discussion between the two began, him on the road and our potential suicide at the top of the story Bridge, between two radios connected to the turntable. I was able to convince him that proper use of the two-way radio could best be achieved by foot pressure in the basket that was suspended at the top of the turntable ladder. This brought him into the basket, I followed very quickly and gave the order, "bring us down fast." Within seconds, we were back on the bitumen and the young man, who by now was probably emotionally spent and passive, was escorted away by the police. I got a short letter from the deputy chief officer in response to my report telling me that I "carried out the rescue in a most efficient manner. Well done."

I can tell you that the city in the early hours of the morning from the top of the story Bridge is quite spectacular. The lights are something to be seen. However, you do have to be careful of the crosswind.

Chapter 18. A Fire Service Review (before and after).

STATISTICS MAKE IT POSSIBLE TO LOOK at changes to the Brisbane fire service since it has been taken over by the Queensland government. These are statistics that are a matter of record and cannot be denied.

In 1989 Brisbane had a population of 774, 557 and it had 21 fire stations. Today, Brisbane's population is over 2 million and it has 20 fire stations. One of the problems with this is the fact that all fire stations in Brisbane have a number; Kemp Place is number one, Roma Street number two, et cetera. Hamilton station and Nundah station were closed down and one station, Hendra, was built in the middle of these two. This meant that in the numbering system we no longer had a station number six. This has been overcome by numbering a new station outside of Brisbane. A station has been built at Redland Bay which carries the number six, hence we now have a number six station but it's not in Brisbane.

Apart from the number of stations, there has been a reduction in the number of pumps at major stations. Kemp Place has been reduced from three pumps to two, Roma Street has been reduced from three pumps to two, Windsor station has been reduced from two pumps to one, and Annerley station has been reduced from two pumps to one. Further, the crews on some of these pumps have been reduced from one officer and 5 to 1 officer and three. Brisbane no longer has a pump with a crew of one and five. In total, over the last 20 to 30 years, while the city of Brisbane was mushrooming to more than double its population, the fire service in Brisbane has had a reduction in operational numbers of over 20%.

When I was the duty officer at Kemp Place fire station at start of shift I would have a parade of oncoming personnel. I would call for three ranks knowing that I would have approximately 30 men. If you went to Kemp Place now and counted heads you might count seven or eight. There has been in recent times some media attention in the Whiskey-a-go-go fire in St Paul's Terrace, which claimed 15 lives. If that fire happened today, the Brisbane fire service could not mount the same response as it did in the 1970s.

The Brisbane Fire Brigade badge carried a motto, "Semper Paratus", which means always ready. The Brisbane Fire Brigade always tried to make sure that we lived up to that motto. The new badge for the Queensland Fire Service carries no motto at all. When you look at the available resources, the previous motto would certainly not be appropriate.

In recent times, Sandgate fire station has been closed and another station has opened at Bracken Ridge. The station at Sandgate was in the middle of the town, was a couple of doors from the police station, was very close to schools, and was very close (about two minutes) to a large facility for caring for the elderly. The station at Bracken Ridge is in the middle of a suburb and a long way removed from institutions listed above.

Northlakes, on the north side of Brisbane in the newly established shire of Moreton, could be described as a satellite city. Apart from the ever expanding suburban sprawl, it has one of the largest shopping complexes in the south-east corner. The Shire of Moreton, combining previous shires of Redcliffe, Caboolture, and Pine Rivers, is fast approaching a population of half a million and will soon overtake the population of the state of Tasmania. When the area of Northlakes was first booming, I noticed a new police station and a new ambulance station in the middle of this new suburb and close to the shopping centre. I rang the local member of Parliament at that time, Dean Wells, and basically said, where is the fire station? He replied that he would get back to me. He did, informing me of plans to build a fire station at Burpengary. The response time from the proposed new station at Burpengary to Northlakes would be completely unacceptable to a professional fire service. In any case, I visited that station and spoke to the officer in charge, an old workmate of mine, and he told me that they did not respond to anything in Northlakes but in fact they were looking after the booming area of Burpengary and backing up Caboolture.

So where does the response come from for Northlakes? The nearest station that could respond is Petrie. Petrie station, before the rapid expansion that has occurred all around it, originally had three appliances, one professional appliance, one auxiliary appliance, and an emergency tender. That's more than Petrie station has now. When this station was operating as the Pine Rivers Fire Brigade, there was no development west of the state school on Dayboro road, in fact nothing but vegetation on the western side of the school until you got to Dayboro. On the eastern side of Petrie, there was no development east of Kalangur until you got to Rothwell. As we move into the area previously under the responsibility of the Redcliffe Fire Brigade, we notice the change in available fire service response in that area. Redcliffe Fire Brigade used to have a substantial two story fire station in the middle of Redcliffe, within reasonable response distance to the Redcliffe Hospital and the industrial estate. It also had an engine room allowing for multiple appliances and a purposeful training facility at the rear of the station. That station has been shut down, I believe given away, and a new single bay, one pump station has been built close to the marina on the extreme north of what was once Redcliffe Shire.

Many country fire brigades suffered similar reductions. Warwick Fire Brigade, for example, operated a full-time professional fire service, 24 hours a day. After it became part of the Queensland fire service, it lost half of its professional service to an auxiliary service. Civic minded citizens who become auxiliary firefighters are usually members of the community occupied in a number of professions; e.g. the local shopkeeper, electrician, et cetera. This means when they receive a call on their pager they hurry to the station, await the rest of the crew, and then turn out. Consequently, the response time to the emergency may be three times what we might expect from a professional service who immediately responds from the station. Warwick has only just recently been able to return to a fully professional service, 24 hours a day. During the interim years, there were two fatalities in separate incidents late at night at house fires. When responding to a house fire emergency, the attendance time (the time taken to arrive at the emergency after the alarm) is the most important factor in the possibility of a life rescue.

Small brigades on the outskirts of Brisbane on both sides of the river would call upon assistance from Brisbane in the event of something beyond their normal capacity. This was established practice and it was at a time when we could afford to assist such brigades without seriously reducing our own resources. The circumstances we have now are that the fire service in these outer areas that are now part of the Queensland fire service, but used to be the local Fire Brigade, has been reduced in capacity and so has Brisbane itself.

On a personal level, each individual firefighter was issued with a uniform; that is to say, boots, work clothes, turnout gear (helmet, turnout coat, and attached belt with axe), and dress uniform including trousers, dress shirts, tie, tunic and cap. The only people who receive a dress uniform these days are the senior ranks. Having a uniform has become a privilege of rank under this fire service management.

Anybody might ask, how is all this to be paid for? In the case of Brisbane, before there was a Queensland fire service or a Fire Brigade levy, the Brisbane fire service was funded by insurance companies collectively. From the details that I have given here, the fire service, the personnel and the citizens of Brisbane received more then than they do now.

We should look at the revenue that is supposed to pay for this essential service. A Fire Brigade levy was first introduced by Peter Beattie, who was premier at that time. It is now called an emergency services Levy. Before this change, whether or not a property was obliged to pay this levy depended on whether or not a reticulated water supply was available. Once it became an emergency services Levy it was possible to increase the number of properties from which the tax could be collected, thus increasing the amount of revenue. This may also mean that the government of the day has more scope in deciding how to spend the money. I am not able to determine the exact amount of money that this tax (a levy is after all a tax by another name) acquires. It is possible, however, to speculate about the numbers.

Every ratepayer in Brisbane and the surrounding areas pays this identifiable levy in their rates amounting to approximately $50 with every rate notice. The population of Brisbane is over 2 million, and the population of the Moreton Shire is approaching half a million. I am not familiar with the other areas immediately surrounding Brisbane, and the population of the Gold Coast is probably close to rivalling Brisbane. We could safely say that the population of the area in the south-east corner is probably around 5 million people. Of course, cities to the north of us like Townsville, Cairns, Gladstone, et cetera would be similarly taxed. If we simply concentrate on an estimate of 5 million people in the south-east corner we could estimate that 1.25 million rate notices might be issued in this area. This would amount to a revenue of approximately $250 million per year in the south-east corner alone. How much of this levy is spent on the fire service I do not know. I do know that in Brisbane, the city, the fire service, and the staff were much better off before the Queensland Fire Service was established than it is now. It may be that the total staff level in Brisbane has increased; there are probably many people now who ride comfortable chairs in air-conditioned offices and less people who ride red trucks to emergencies. The emergencies, however, the areas where we have to perform to look after people and property, cannot be dealt with from air-conditioned offices; when the proverbial hits the fan unpredictably as it often does in our society, it has to be dealt with by people who ride red trucks.

Chapter 19. A Summary.

THIS IS THE REMINISCING CHAPTER. I had the chance to work with many good men of all ranks, and I am grateful for their acquaintance, their assistance, and their support. Many of these men still meet on the first Monday of every month at a bowling club in Lawnton; men of all ranks enjoying each other's company, from Commissioner Lee Johnson to rank and file firemen. They greet each other as friends, swap stories (some true, some embellished) and look forward to their next meeting.

As for me, I can divide my service into two parts, the Metropolitan Fire Brigade part and the Q FS part. The MFB part is remembered as efficient, decent, honourable and honest. The Q FS part, unfortunately, was full of political intrigue. Men were promoted not on merit but because of their willingness to do and say whatever their political masters demanded. Our ability to perform was considerably reduced, both on a turnout basis and in backup and support. There were of course, some senior promotions who were deserving and did not fall into the political net. Thank God we had them.

I can make claim to some history.

My Ethical and Diligence Medal with three bars.

My National Service Medal.

The Queen's Long Service And Good Conduct Medal.

I was the last president of the Metropolitan Fire Brigade officers Association, due to a fraudulent amalgamation ballot.

I was the only president of the MFBOA who was not promoted to the senior ranks (it was considered that if you were elected to the presidency of the Officers Association, you had the confidence, respect and trust of your fellow officers and you had displayed the ability to manage and lead).

I had more charges laid against me than any other officer in the history of the fire service, and I managed to survive.

I am the owner of a piece of political history: – Citizens Right of Reply number one, by Bruce Wilkinson.

I am in possession of assurances by two consecutive fire service Commissioners that I will not be discriminated against; unfortunately some senior officers totally ignored these assurances.

On my operational record, I am able to say that I did not have what we classify as a failure; none of my crew were seriously injured, none of the people that I had to rescue died or suffered any serious injury because of some mistake that I made. This is certainly the most important part of my service, the endorsement of our purpose and existence. At fires both structural and bush, I did a reasonable job of extinction and preservation. After every emergency, it was my practice to assemble the staff that attended and have a debrief. This was theoretically to enable us to discuss what actions we took, could we have done it differently, and how successful we were. We did carry out such a discussion but it also gave every crew member the chance to express their feelings and relieve themselves of some inner tensions, especially after attendance at a motor vehicle accident.

I have an apology to make. When I retired, my workmates gave me a retirement party; the Taigum tavern gave us the use of their beer garden for the night.

From my workmates on my retirement.

On such an occasion it is expected that the centre of attention, me, would make a speech. It was the worst speech in our history, ridiculously brief and hardly qualifying as a speech at all. The men who attended deserved much better and I do apologise. In fact, by the time I got to this point, having survived God knows how many attacks and having to engineer my survival on a number of occasions, I was mentally burnt out.

I was able to outlast most of the people who tried to bring me down, watching their departure as they were obliged to leave.

On the other hand, I was able to retire at a time of my choosing.

Regrets? Not many, but a few. I do not have any regrets about anything that I did, I have some regrets about what I did not do or possibly should have done. I should have opposed the amalgamation ballot which destroyed the MFBOA. I was too trusting of the people who carried it out and I had too much faith in the process. If I had opposed it from my position as president, it would not have happened and the amalgamation would not have occurred, leaving the MFBOA still in existence. There were occasions when I should have taken what is usually described as affirmative action. There were occasions when I could have taken some of my enemies in the senior ranks to the Industrial Commission to make them accountable for their actions; I was in fact not aggressive enough and too forgiving.

My dress for memorial service. I served under all these badges.

I have a wish list.
- I would like to see The Fire Service Act repaired to the standard that it was when it was first introduced.

- I would like to see the fire service brought back up to the standard that I encountered when I first joined the service in 1967.
- I would like to see all ranks issued with a uniform; I don't believe a uniform should be a privilege for senior ranks only.
- Of course, I would like to finally be paid the superannuation money that was stolen from me at the point of my retirement.
- I have a brass helmet, but it is not the one I was issued.

An MFB brass helmet. (I used to wear one.)

The brass helmet that was issued to me in 1967 has some numbers on the inside at the back. The size of the helmet, 7 1/4 (some people said I was big headed) and my brigade number, 114. If anybody has that helmet, I would gladly trade the helmet I have for the one that I was issued with. I would even consider a small reward for the exchange.

Some people ponder their chosen profession and may regret their choice. Not me. I believe, having the opportunity to save lives and rescue people, save people's property, and work with the finest men that our society has produced, was not only the right choice but a privilege.

www.ingramcontent.com/pod-product-compliance
Lightning Source LLC
LaVergne TN
LVHW011727060526
838200LV00051B/3056